# BOMBARDED NAPLES SINGS

## Piero Bellanova

Translated and with an introduction by
Christopher Adams

*t*

Published by
Troubador Publishing Ltd
9 Priory Business Park
Kibworth
Leicester LE8 0RX, UK
Tel: (+44) 0116 279 2299
Email: books@troubador.co.uk
Web: www.troubador.co.uk


Series Editor
George Ferzoco

Front cover: Gerardo Dottori, *Aerial Battle above the Gulf of Naples*; or, *Inferno of Aerial Battle above the Paradise of the Gulf, 1942*, oil on board, 200 x 150 cm, Milan: private collection (courtesy Archivio Gerardo Dottori Associazione Culturale).

9781788039413

# Foreword

Reading the introduction to Adams' English version of Piero Bellanova's poem, it quickly becomes apparent that the translator is intimately aquainted with Italian Futurism. More importantly, perhaps, since the text was published in 1943, he has an unusually fine grasp of Futurist developments during the tumultuous 1940s. Although this period has received little attention from scholars, he has investigated it in detail and manages to recreate the poem's original context. This in turn enables the reader to understand numerous references both to fellow Futurists and to contemporary events in Italy.

Not only is the book's introduction an excellent piece of scholarship by itself, but it also prepares the reader for the lengthy poem that follows. Adams' knowledge of Italian and of Futurist texts in general enables him to closely recreate the original work. Undaunted by numerous idiosyncracies associated with Futurism, he finds precisely the right words to translate Bellanova's linguistic acrobatics into English. While occasional passages can be demanding, they are consistently translated with sensitivity and with brio. As a result, English speakers will discover both a new world and a new poet.

**Willard Bohn**
**Professor Emeritus of French and Comparative Literature**
**Illinois State University, USA**

# An Originalità Speciaaale[1]
# Piero Bellanova's
# *Bombarded Naples Sings*

## Christopher Adams

Intensely lyrical, unabashedly sensual and infused with *attualità bruciante*,[2] *Bombarded Naples Sings* is a minor masterpiece of Italian Futurist literature. The final volume to appear under the movement's illustrious Edizioni Futuriste di 'Poesia' imprint – which had published some of the most significant works in the history of the literary avant garde over the course of the preceding thirty-eight years[3] – it was a product of Futurism's concluding (and undoubtedly least studied) phase, extending from Italy's entry into World War Two in 1940 to the death of the movement's leader, F. T. Marinetti, in December 1944.

First published in August 1943[4] – between the fall of Mussolini's Fascist regime in July, and the invasion of the Italian mainland by Allied troops that September – it has been seen as an attempt "to construct an epic of everyday life by means of a first-hand account of the war".[5] However, the ultimate purpose of this frequently moving work would appear to have been of a consolatory, 'spiritual' nature, offering a means by which Bellanova and his readers might, if only temporarily, "escape the terrible devastation of our adored Italy through Art".[6] With its elegiac tone and precise, vividly imagistic language, *Bombarded Naples Sings* challenges stereotypical notions as to the grandiloquent, florid character of Futurist poetry, and illustrates that even in these later years the movement's literary works were "much more diverse (and much more interesting) than this caricature would suggest".[7]

# I.    Italian Futurism in the 1940s

It is a widely held belief that "Futurism had run out of steam"[8] by 1940, having been in existence for more than three decades.[9] Consequently, the movement's output during the war years still awaits the comprehensive consideration which has been given to the other phases of so-called *secondo futurismo*, spanning the 1920s and 1930s.[10] During those years Futurism had grown into a mass movement with representatives working in almost every conceivable creative sphere, from fashion to photography, ceramics, advertising and even cuisine. By contrast, the 1940s witnessed a fall in membership[11] and a renewed focus on painting and poetry – the movement's initial areas of interest. However, a perception of creeping atrophy only partly accounts for the marginalization of this phase in Futurist scholarship. An altogether more serious obstacle to its positive reception is the widespread conviction that "Futurist production of the 1940s [was] little more than Fascist war propaganda".[12] As is well known, the movement had definitively aligned itself with Mussolini's regime around 1924, its painters and poets going on to eulogize the Duce in an endless stream of works throughout the *ventennio*.[13] Yet Futurism's continued endorsement of Fascism in what was undoubtedly its darkest and most brutal hour has led to this final phase being seen as "an epilogue [...] of the most unsavoury kind".[14] Many scholars have also pointed to the deleterious aesthetic consequences of the movement's apparent compromise with the forces of reaction and conservatism at this time, maintaining that Futurist imagery inevitably drifted toward the kind of 'kitsch' that Clement Greenberg identified as being typical of art favoured by political regimes, in a seminal essay of 1939.[15] The figurative, war-related 'aeropaintings' that featured in state-sponsored exhibitions between 1941 and 1943 are often considered emblematic in this respect, such imagery being seen as having debased a genre that had previously explored the visual novelties and metaphysical dimensions of flight in a lyrical, and stylistically heterogeneous, manner.[16]

However, just as the 1940s cannot be said to have witnessed a rupture in the ideological foundations of the movement, it is also a rarely acknowledged fact that much of the work produced during this period was in no way aesthetically unchallenging or retrogressive (despite its political dimensions, and the individual beliefs of its creators), remaining open to influences from

Italy's wider cultural panorama and/or reflecting Futurism's own stylistic ancestry.

In terms of the visual arts, the imagery of painters such as Alfredo Gauro Ambrosi, Sante Monachesi and Tato (Guglielmo Sansoni) was shot through with an expressionist charge recalling the contemporary work of Renato Guttuso and the artists of the Corrente group, of which the Futurists were most certainly aware.[17] Likewise, the imagery of other 'aeropainters of war' such as Verossì (Albino Siviero) or Tullio Crali[18] cannot be dismissed as pedestrian realism, given its incorporation of multiple perspectives, unnatural or exaggerated colours, and fluid extension of forms in space in order to convey the plunging, vertiginous sensations and 'states of mind' experienced by pilots. Different again are Angelo Caviglioni's evocations of aerial warfare, being (abstract) expressionist *tours de force* that focus less on depicting the machines engaged in conflict than on the clashing waves of energy generated by their struggle.

Furthermore, it would be misleading to suggest that Futurist art of the 1940s was synonymous with such *aeropittura di guerra*. Enrico Prampolini – undoubtedly the most significant artist to be associated with the movement during these later years[19] – continued to pursue his long-standing interest in "the kingdoms of the microcosm and the macrocosm",[20] producing distinctive imagery in which biomorphic elements floating in limitless spaces vividly suggest liberation from the earth's gravitational pull and humanity's attainment of the weightless realms of the cosmos. Important links were also forged with Como's contingent of 'concrete' abstractionists, whose crystalline, self-contained and exquisitely balanced geometric compositions were to bring an entirely new dimension to Futurist exhibitions at this time.[21]

Futurist literature of the 1940s likewise resists what Cinzia Sartini Blum has described as "reductionist and dismissive critical gestures".[22] After an admittedly somewhat inauspicious start, certain of the movement's poets went on to formulate invigorating ideas which imparted a dramatic forward momentum to Futurism through their attempts to anticipate the defining characteristics of verbal communication in post-war society.

Just as aeropainting continued to play a significant role in Futurist art, so too

**Fig. 1**   Piero Bellanova (right) with Enrico Prampolini.

'aeropoetry' remained a key genre within Futurist literature between 1940 and 1943.[23] These expressions of the 'aerial' sensibility had followed a similar trajectory over the course of the preceding decade – the movement's poets having interpreted the concept of terrestrial transcendence in both a literal and a metaphysical sense, in the same manner as their colleagues working in the sphere of the visual arts. During the 1940s, the concerns of *aeropoesia* continued to parallel those of *aeropittura*, revealing a greater stress on military subject matter.[24] Aeropoetry has tended to be seen as something of a backward step, formally speaking, insofar as it reinstated the use of a single typeface and the traditional linear page grid – two conventions that had been swept aside by Marinetti's 'typographical revolution' of 1913.[25] Additionally, the brutal dismemberment of grammar and syntax characteristic of Futurism's earlier 'words in freedom' poetry (*parole in libertà*) was significantly tempered in the *parole più o meno in libertà*[26] of aeropoetry, with its "(partial) recuperation of syntactic and narrative structures".[27] One might reasonably expect there to have been an explosive re-emergence of the more robust *parole in libertà* technique during the war years, given that it had initially been conceived as a means of exploring "zone[s] of intense life (revolution, war [...] and so on)";[28] yet curiously this did not happen, save for a few rather rudimentary exercises in that 'free expressive orthography' likewise outlined in Marinetti's early manifestos.[29] Stylistically at odds with its violent subject matter, often tainted by Fascist rhetoric and occasionally blighted by sentimentality,[30] *aeropoesia di guerra* undoubtedly remains the most incongruous and least satisfying of the poetic forms proposed by the Futurists during the 1940s.

However, two inherently *anti*-rhetorical forms of poetry emerged toward the end of this phase (1943-44), one of which emphasized the visual dimension of the written word, while the other investigated the expressive potential of sound. Although differing in these respects, they nevertheless shared a concern with identifying "certain necessities of language" that would be "made evident by existence following the war".[31]

Born of a conviction that "to see will become more necessary than to listen",[32] Carlo Belloli's pioneering *poesia visuale* anticipated many of the features of later 'concrete' poetry in its extreme economy of means and conception of poetic compositions as objects "to be visualized before being read for their meaning".[33] In direct contrast to this – and to Belloli's rigorously cerebral approach to language – Crali and Marinetti proposed an abstract-expressionist form of poetry which they termed *parole musicali* ('musical words'), grounded in the unrestrained use of onomatopoeia and employment of neologisms "invented and modulated by the poet".[34] By these means they intended to recover something of the flexibility, universality[35] and intuitive, primal power possessed by vocal sounds prior to the development of structured languages, which had imposed restrictive "prescribed meanings" on them ("in issuing his first cries, primitive man instinctively created certain noises that had a direct relationship with the phenomena to which they referred").[36] Of course, such ideas had already been explored in those 'transrational' (*zaum*) works produced by the Russian avant garde during the early years of the century.[37] However, like Belloli's proto-concrete experiments, this call for a linguistic *tabula rasa* seems to have reflected a wider apprehension on the part of those Futurists working during the 1940s that they occupied the cusp of two very different eras, and that their new task was to prognosticate the expressive conventions of an as yet embryonic post-war world. Certainly, Prampolini was aware of the transitional nature of this period, as a text of 1944 illustrates:

Whilst mechanical civilization has exhausted its ethical and historical role, having reached its ultimate point in the current conflagration, one can discern the advent of a new civilization – the *scientific civilization* – toward which we have looked with faith for some time as innovatory artists [...].[38]

Accordingly, whilst the cataclysmic events of 1943-44 were ultimately to seal Futurism's fate, they also served to liberate the imaginations of Marinetti and his followers, reawakening the movement's original, visionary spirit, and inspiring a final burst of creativity that anticipated "the future of Futurism".[39]

★★★

*Bombarded Naples Sings* does not fit neatly into any of the above literary categories or genres. Although Marinetti described its author as an "illustrious young aeropoet" in the extraordinary stream of consciousness that constituted his introduction to the text,[40] Bellanova's compositions tend to eschew the exuberant, free-associative character of *aeropoesia*, emphasizing instead the power of the carefully selected word or image. This distinction may partly be explained by the fact that Bellanova was not a poet by vocation, and was therefore perhaps more concerned with following his own poetic inclinations than with mastering the latest stylistic trends. Such a stance might appear paradoxical given his affiliation with a movement that was defined by its dedication to artistic novelty, and which ostensibly insisted that its painters and poets adopt those 'official' aesthetic principles published in its numerous programmatic statements. However, in the final analysis "Futurism was not a formal problem".[41] If its products were 'Futurist' they were so more by virtue of each artist or writer's commitment to the movement as an "attitude to life"[42] than by his or her allegiance to a specific painterly vocabulary or poetic form. As Bellanova's associate Luigi Scrivo[43] asserted in 1941, Futurism was "correctly" understood by its members to be

> a movement in the broadest sense [of the term], affecting wide swathes of the population, where each individual working in the sphere of poetry, literature [or] the arts can express himself *with the utmost freedom* [...].[44]

**6**

Such convictions had been a consistent feature of Futurist ideology throughout the movement's lifespan, as illustrated by a manifesto of 1919 in which the ideal Futurist painter or poet was characterized, in the least prescriptive terms possible, as "one who thinks and expresses himself with originality, force, vivacity, enthusiasm, clarity, simplicity, agility and synthesis".[45] On this basis, there is no doubting the Futurist credentials of either *Bombarded Naples Sings* or its author.

## II.   Piero Bellanova: Life, Times and Work

Bellanova was born on 5 February 1917 in Sant'Agata di Esaro – a small town in rural Calabria, surrounded by the peaks of the southern Apennines – and died in Rome on 19 May 1987. He spent his childhood and early adolescence in Calabria before completing his secondary education at schools in Frascati (Villa Sora) and Cava de' Tirreni in the province of Salerno, where he studied at the *liceo classico* attached to the Abbey of the Holy Trinity.

In 1935, Bellanova enrolled in the Faculty of Medicine at the University of Rome where he specialized in aesthetic surgery. During his studies he also worked at the National Research Council's[46] Institute of Psychology, and organized the first psychotechnical centres for the screening and selection of military personnel – experiences that would prove to be significant in terms of the subsequent orientation of his medical career.

Around this time he encountered Marinetti and became active in the capital's Futurist circles. He also promoted the movement in his native region, publishing a small number of polemical articles in the journal *Calabria Fascista* between 1937 and 1938[47] in which he defended Futurism's aesthetic and ideological character with the zeal typical of a convert.

As previously noted, Bellanova's own work did not slavishly adhere to Futurism's technical recommendations. However, in late 1939 he was a co-signatory (with Marinetti and Scrivo) of a programmatic manifesto which set out the principles of a new literary genre, that of the 'synthetic novel'.[48] Urging the rejection of detailed realism in favour of a poetically concise form of prose, the text proclaimed: "In a century when it is possible to travel at 700km per hour [...] we have nothing but scorn for the depressing monotony of the thousand pages of a Thomas Mann or a Jules Romains", thereby reasserting Futurism's long-standing belief in the virtue of brevity ("*It's stupid to write one hundred pages where one would do*").[49] The following year Bellanova published his own synthetic novel, *Nose-diving into Love*.[50] The first of only two *romanzi sintetici* ever to be published,[51] it incorporated episodes from battles fought in the Tembien region of Ethiopia during 1936 as part of Italy's colonial invasion of the country, as well scenes of derring-do set during the Spanish Civil War. It also succinctly traced the development of the relationship between the novel's two protagonists – the swaggering pilot Enzo and the sporty Adriana – from their first encounter at the *Exhibition of Italian Mineralogical Autarky* (1938-39)[52] to their marriage, condensing around four highly eventful years into just fifteen terse pages. These read like storyboards where the key events of the drama are merely sketched out, thereby fulfilling the requirement that the synthetic novel should be "DYNAMIC [and] SIMULTANEOUS that is to say cinematographic [and] suited to being filmed".[53] To satisfy those readers who found such minimalism disconcerting – or who lacked the ability to "suppose the logical development of the action",[54] having grown accustomed to authors explaining every twist and turn of their plots – Bellanova appended a detailed 'Passéist Contents Page' to the end of his text, where it was indicated how "without adding a single [significant] new episode one might develop this simultaneous synthetic novel into one of the usual analytical epics".[55] *Nose-diving into Love* received a broadly favourable response from the critics, a review in the influential magazine *Domus* describing it as "the novel of modern, Futurist, youth accustomed to swift warfare, a dynamic lifestyle, immediacy and the rapid succession of events".[56]

After graduating in 1941, Bellanova became Marinetti's personal physician and continued to participate in Futurist events, certain of which testified to his newfound confidence as a poet. On 14 January that year he was one of several Futurist writers who declaimed their works at the *finissage* of an exhibition of war paintings by Sante Monachesi in Rome (Fig. 2).[57] Little over a week later he once again collaborated with Marinetti and Scrivo, joining them to demonstrate against a performance of *Our Town* (1938) by the American playwright Thornton Wilder at Rome's Teatro Argentina.[58] Their protest, "conducted [...] in the best tradition of Futurist Action Theatre",[59]

**MOSTRA D'ARTE MONACHESI**

**HOSTARIA**
DELL' **ORSO**

ROMA - VIA MONTE BRIANZO 93
TELEF. 52938

L'AEROPOETA FUTURISTA
**MARINETTI**
SANSEPOLCRISTA ACCADEMICO DI
ITALIA PRESENTERÀ IN DUE MINUTI
**L'AEROPOESIA DI GUERRA**
ALLA CHIUSURA DELLA MOSTRA
DEI BOMBARDAMENTI LONDINESI
E AFRICANI DELL'AEROPITTORE FUTU-
RISTA SANTE MONACHESI
DECLAMERANNO LE LORO AERO-
POESIE DI GUERRA
**MARINETTI - BELLANOVA
- SCRIVO - PATTAROZZI -
MONACHESI -** SIG.NE **NUMERICO
- MARIA GORETTI - DINA CUCINI
:: :: :: PARISELLA :: :: ::**
ORE 19 DEL GIORNO 14 GENNAIO
S i e t e   i n v i t a t o

**Fig. 2** Invitation to the *finissage* of an exhibition of war paintings by Sante Monachesi at Rome's Hostaria dell'Orso, 14 January 1941.

interrupted the play and denounced Wilder for his failure to acknowledge the Futurist ancestry of certain stylistic conceits (the script for *Our Town* specifies that it is to be performed with minimal scenery and props). Yet it was also targeted at the Italian theatrical establishment itself, which Marinetti and his cohorts assailed for what they perceived to be its complacent neglect of radical, home-grown talent in favour of lesser, foreign, imitators – an accusation that was not without a political edge. Defending his actions, Marinetti stated that they were intended

> to denounce the shameless plagiarism of Futurism's technical inventions and to strike a further blow against the stupid and

repugnant snobbish xenomania of a public that is ready to applaud the apparent originality of non-Italian authors without remembering authentic and creative Italian originality [...] The lesson given by us was directed at passéists of every kind Its aim was to assert the inventive importance of Futurist synthetic theatre the only and decisive theatrical revolution of this century[60]

In 1942 Bellanova trained to become a medical officer at the prestigious and pioneering Scuola di Applicazione di Sanità Militare, established in Florence in 1883 and based in a former convent in the north-east of the city, near Piazza San Marco;[61] having completed the course, he was sent to Naples the following year where he undertook his military service.

Again, Bellanova's Futurist activities continued alongside his professional commitments. In 1942 he undersigned a manifesto concerning typography that reaffirmed the continued relevance of Futurism's earlier innovations in this sphere, asserting: "Given the dramatic immediacy required by the battlefield the pages of our Futurist synthetic novels and [...] newspapers [...] will be comparable to Futurist cityscapes [with] illuminated signs marching upwards".[62] To a limited extent, such ideas had been reflected in the modestly unconventional spacing and differently weighted typefaces of *Nose-diving into Love*. However, the efficacy of Bellanova's writing was in no sense reliant on such visual effects, which are almost entirely absent from the present volume.

In January 1943 he contributed a truncated (or perhaps preliminary) version of his poem 'Bombarded Naples Sings' to the *Amorous Bellicose Futurist Songbook*, a bizarre and somewhat motley anthology of 'lyrics' written by Futurist poets, or adapted from existing compositions.[63] According to its editors, these aimed to arouse optimism and patriotic sentiment, combating the prevailing melancholy spirit of popular song, which only encouraged "neurasthenia cowardice or egotistical [political] absenteeism".[64] Bellanova also participated in the so-called 'Propagandizing Dynamisms of War Poetry' – a series of public recitals launched that February by the National Union of Authors and Writers (of which Marinetti was Secretary).[65] The second such event – intended "to stimulate indispensable Italian pride with beautiful musical images"[66] – was held in Rome on 31 May 1943,[67] on which occasion

Bellanova read two compositions from his forthcoming anthology *Bombarded Naples Sings* that were described by the correspondent of *Il Popolo di Trieste* as "original and well received".[68]

★★★

It would appear that Bellanova was working on at least two other texts during the war years – the preliminary pages of *Bombarded Naples Sings* advertising the "imminent publication" of a second synthetic novel optimistically titled *The Great Future*, and what would seem to have been an encyclopaedia or historical overview of the Futurist movement, written in collaboration with Scrivo;[69] he also continued to write poetry.[70] In the immediate post-war period, certain Futurists were keen to regroup, reconnect and resume their work. Yet the practical obstacles to any such plans were formidable, as the architect Alberto Sartoris noted in a letter to Crali of 26 July 1946:

> I have many things to tell you about a new artistic group that I would like to put together, but how is this to be done now that we have all been scattered to the four winds? It would be necessary to see each other regularly in order to define our exact position and our future activity. [...] I may be able to organize some exhibitions abroad, but it will only be possible to overcome the serious customs issues involved once peace is established.[71]

Futurism's previous ideological affiliations also made any attempt to re-launch the movement problematic, as Crali himself noted, observing that its works had become "like truffles – it's rare to find them, and they stink (because they are 'Fascist', according to journalistic criticism)".[72]

Moreover, it soon became apparent that no consensus existed among the surviving Futurists as to the best way forward. Once their immediate post-war sense of disorientation abated, many were reluctant to revive the movement, given that its aesthetic innovations and lessons were already being taken in interesting new directions by emerging schools and artistic tendencies. Some welcomed this process of diffusion, and even actively engaged with younger artists who acknowledged the inspiration of Futurist ideas in their work.[73] Other figures adapted less well, being unable – or unwilling – to negotiate the paradigm shift that had taken place in Italian culture, and fiercely resisted what they saw as the disembodied, de-contextualized reincarnation of Futurist principles. For them, their movement remained the pioneering avant garde *par excellence*, one that was able to incorporate and assimilate new associations, artists and aesthetics, but which could never be assimilated or absorbed itself. These figures were united in their belief that Futurism could outlive the tragedy of the Second World War just as it had the First, maintaining that it remained a relevant, revolutionary force in contemporary culture. In his memoirs, Crali describes the Futurist 'summit' of 26 February 1950 that brought these conflicting attitudes to a head:

> Futurist meeting in Milan. Those present are Buzzi, Mazza, Benedetta (Cappa),[74] Masnata, Crali, Scurto, Acquaviva, Munari and Andreoni. Benedetta's intention to archive the movement, declaring it finished, quickly becomes apparent. The workshop is closed! There are those who for one reason or another think this would be a good idea – the spent forces, the dead weights, the speculators. I rebel in the clearest possible terms: "[...] Marinetti has gone but the Futurists remain! If you wish to become bourgeois then so be it. I'm carrying on!" The meeting closes: the Movement falls to pieces, Futurism continues. [...] A wretched and ridiculous end for a bunch of anti-traditionalist revolutionaries.[75]

Bellanova appears to have stood aloof from such debates, although he maintained contact with certain of his former Futurist colleagues throughout his life.[76] He also continued to move in cultural circles. In 1945 he co-founded a society named Il Convito, which organized weekly events in Rome concerning the arts and sciences, and the following year he married Anna Madami, a niece of the painter Mario Sironi.

In 1946, Bellanova's medical expertise was called upon by the Ministry for the Constituent Assembly – a body which sought to establish the foundations of a new Italian Constitution in the aftermath of the Second World War – when he was appointed Secretary of the Sub-Commission for Health.[77] Thereafter, his energies were increasingly directed toward establishing a professional career in the field of psychology – an area of research that had fascinated him from an early age, as we have seen – and during the 1950s he trained as a psychoanalyst under the pioneering yet idiosyncratic Emilio Servadio,[78] one of the keys figures in the establishment of the Società Psicoanalitica Italiana (SPI). The relationship between psychoanalysis and art constituted one aspect of Bellanova's research, and he was particularly interested in how the filmmaking process reflected certain principles of psychoanalytic theory. In 1964 he acted as a consultant on Paolo Spinola's film *La Fuga* (*The Escape*) which – through flashbacks and dream sequences laden with Freudian symbolism – chronicles the breakdown of a young woman named Piera, whose emotional problems stem from her strained relationship with her parents, and are compounded by her unfulfilling marriage and repressed homosexual urges. In 1980 he also contributed an introductory text to a volume concerning psychoanalysis and Italian cinema.[79]

Over the course of his career Bellanova became an acknowledged authority in his field, as well as a respected criminologist, and occupied prominent official roles within the SPI from the late 1960s onward.[80] Today he is considered to be "one of the fathers of psychoanalysis in Italy".[81]

## III.  *Bombarded Naples Sings*: Themes and Characteristics

Despite its title, *Bombarded Naples Sings* was not inspired solely by Bellanova's experiences as a medical officer stationed in the city during 1943, and is in no sense a poetic counterpart to Norman Lewis's celebrated wartime memoir *Naples '44*.[82] Episodes dating from Bellanova's time there are evoked in its pages, but so too are friendships forged during his training at the Scuola di Applicazione di Sanità Militare in Florence, as well as real or imagined flights above Venice, summertime visits to the Adriatic resorts of Pula and Brijuni, and excursions into the mountains around Trento. Evidently, it was the poems themselves – rather than their thematic content – that Bellanova wished to dedicate to Naples out of affection for, and solidarity with, one of the most heavily bombed Italian cities of World War Two.[83]

In this context, it is significant to note that whilst defiant and intensely patriotic, *Bombarded Naples Sings* never lapses into polemics (except perhaps in the volume's title poem), and is free from any admiring references to Fascism or expressions of *fede in Mussolini*; nowhere does Bellanova's text

**Fig. 3** Piero Bellanova, *Bombarded Naples Sings*
(Rome: Edizioni Futuriste di 'Poesia', 1943); cover design
by Enrico Prampolini (reproduced by kind permission of the artist's heirs).
Image courtesy of L'Arengario Studio Bibliografico.

invoke the Duce as Italy's ultimate protector or deliverer. Realistically, this cannot be accounted for in terms of an eleventh-hour deletion of any eulogistic remarks concerning the regime following its collapse in late July 1943. This would have been far too involved a process to undertake at such a late stage had they formed an integral part of Bellanova's compositions, given that *Bombarded Naples Sings* was published the following month. Moreover, it would have been a pointless exercise, for Futurism's political affiliations were hardly a secret. Rather, Bellanova's poetry was simply not ideologically-driven; even when concerned with current events, the experiences it relates and the emotions it evokes tend to be universal and 'eternal' in character, and it does not require any specific dogmatic allegiance on the part of the reader in order for its sentiments to be understood.

A letter from Bellanova to Crali reveals that he had written a volume of poems by mid-August 1941, although it is unclear whether these formed the basis of the present anthology, published two years later.[84] That there was at least some degree of overlap is suggested by the fact that Bellanova wished to use Crali's painting *Motor, Seducer of Clouds* to illustrate this initial collection of works – believing it to be "attuned to the spirit of some of the poems in my book"[85] – and would later include it in *Bombarded Naples Sings* itself.[86] If some form of correspondence did exist between the two texts (which seems likely, given that no other volume of poetry was published by Bellanova during the years 1941-43) the initial version would have undergone a major structural and conceptual change between the spring of 1942 and its publication the following summer, when Bellanova incorporated a series of moving 'letters' to family members, medical colleagues and Futurist associates.[87] Interposed between the poems – to which they relate in one way or another[88] – these represent one of the most distinctive features of *Bombarded Naples Sings*. If it is evident that Bellanova's poetry was for the most part intended to be read and reflected upon in private,[89] these 'letters' further intensify the volume's sense of intimacy – particularly as many of them are not addressed to public figures, but to close personal friends of the author.[90] Their inclusion may have been inspired by the 'Futurist Manifesto of Wartime Friendship', various versions of which were published between late 1941 and early 1942 by Marinetti and the Neapolitan Futurist Francesco Cangiullo.[91] The text observed how "in this moment, when certain nations are firing at one another, others are being subsumed [and] others are running rampant", friendship was "more indispensable than ever before"; and in fact, *Bombarded Naples Sings* was not the only text to celebrate "the epistolary art of describing the colourful and musical dynamisms of our peninsula" at this time.[92] That Bellanova would have had the opportunity to rethink his initial text and make such changes is indicated in his aforementioned letter to Crali where, with evident frustration, he assured the artist that there would be ample time for him to substitute *Motor, Seducer of Clouds* with one of his images of parachutists, if he so wished, since "although the text is now ready to go and has been paginated the censor is holding everything up because he has not yet given me approval [to proceed]".

In addition to friendship, Bellanova's text addressed those "two great themes"[93] that had (at least theoretically) also constituted the focus of the earlier *Canzoniere futurista amoroso guerriero*: love and war. In the manner of their engagement with the latter subject, his poems were consistent with prevailing Futurist orthodoxy as set out in Marinetti's 1940 manifesto 'New Aesthetic of War'.[94] In it, he had urged his poets to give greater emphasis than ever before to the impersonal, industrial and mechanical aspects of modern warfare, and called for their works to reflect a growing apprehension of the 'autonomy' of aeroplanes, tanks, submarines and torpedo-boats, each possessing their own "personalities" and being "worthy of glory independently of the soldiers contained within". Fulfilling Marinetti's instruction to "describe and hymn the autonomy of trimotors which […] although created by mankind hasten to do battle on their own account not caring a rap for humanity",[95] several of Bellanova's poems describe military engagements as encounters between machines rather than men:

> The torpedo-bomber has pierced
> the horizon's grey silk
> like a tiny inkblot
> on the skysea's damp paper
> made for love letters
>
> Now the propeller announces
> its noisy presence
> to the beautiful steel ship
> with a roaring serenade of war[96]

Bellanova's exploration of carnal matters was similarly aligned with contemporary Futurist thought, engaging with the theme of 'war aphrodisia'[97] in a robust and forthright manner. In fact, the movement had long maintained that conflict modified traditional gender roles and impacted upon sexual mores, Marinetti's experiences during the First World War having led him to conclude that "any self-respecting young woman has at least three lovers in wartime",[98] and to claim that the pressures and stresses of battle made it "necessary to accelerate […] even love".[99] Upon the outbreak of war in 1940 these matters once again became a focus for debate, and the text in which Marinetti had made the above observations was immediately reissued. Swiftly withdrawn by the authorities in the spring of 1941, on the basis that its bawdy content ill-befitted the dignity of a Royal Academician,[100] the volume's ideas were defiantly revisited later that year in Antonino Tullier's manifesto 'Mediterranean Synthetic Love'.[101] The text insisted that romantic encounters could still be "of the most profound nature even if not prolonged over time giving to minutes the value of a day to a month the value of a year thereby destroying the prevailing opinion that associates much time and therefore much paralyzing sentimental nostalgia with acts of love". Such "proud brief intense profound loves of soldiers" – later commended by the *Canzoniere futurista amoroso guerriero*[102] – were the subject of a poem in the present volume titled 'To the Soldiers' Woman':

> I savour the harmonious elasticity
> of your ankles
> while my rough hands
> want to break
> your fragility
> and my parched lips
> gather kisses from your mouth
> like almond blossom
> and fleshy strawberries
>
> I want to wind
> a string of dewdrops
> around your graceful neck
>
> But listen
>
> The attack begins again
>
> Quickly
>
> Give me your luminous heart[103]

An urgent need to seek love among the ruins and escape the devastation of war also characterizes 'Flying over Venice', an altogether more romantic composition. The precision, clarity and sheer beauty of Bellanova's imagery in this poem highlights the qualities that elevate his work above that of many of his peers – a case in point being his comparison of the sun-drenched dome of the Venetian sky, strewn with clouds, to the sparkling cupolas of San Marco and its congregation, dressed in ceremonial attire:

Mosaic gold
pours from the sun
in a single gush
like a sacred anthem
in this glittering cathedral
bathed in liquid blue

Madonnas' perfumes
and infinite clouds of
tender first communion veils[104]

★★★

Despite its evident fascination with the spectacle of modern warfare, and its enthusiastic exploration of the Futurist *estetica della macchina*, *Bombarded Naples Sings* in no way merits the label of "vulgar and inflammatory propaganda"[105] that tends to be applied indiscriminately and simplistically to all of the movement's products dating from the 1940s. Ultimately, it is the redemptive power of art, the majesty of nature, and the transcendent values of love and friendship that emerge as the key themes of the text. It is hoped that the present translation will not only enable Bellanova's poetry to find a wider audience, but that the quiet intensity of this singular little book will encourage others to approach and investigate this unduly neglected and much-maligned phase of Futurist activity with greater objectivity and openness of mind.

This edition of *Bombarded Naples Sings* would not have been possible without the encouragement, help and support of many people. First and foremost, my sincere thanks go to Monica and Patrizia Bellanova for granting me permission to translate their father's work – a long-cherished project of mine – and to Umberto Tarsitano for having facilitated our initial correspondence. I am extremely grateful to George Ferzoco and Jeremy Thompson for their commitment to the project, and to all at Troubador who have worked on this volume. For their invaluable assistance and advice, my sincere thanks also go to Andrea Baffoni, Anna Bartolozzi Crali, Valeria Carullo, Massimo Duranti, Anna Maria Prampolini, Massimo Prampolini, Paolo Tonini, Bernard Vere, Claudia Zanardi and Federico Zanoner.

**Brighton, May 2017**

# Endnotes

1     See F. T. Marinetti, 'Aeropoema-collaudo scritto dal poeta F. T. Marinetti', in Piero Bellanova, *Bombardata Napoli canta* (Rome: Edizioni Futuriste di 'Poesia', 1943), pp. 7-21 (p. 19); see below, pp. 33-43 (p. 41).

2     Literally, 'burning topicality': a term used by F. T. Marinetti to emphasize the cultural and socio-political relevance of his movement's art and literature. See his introduction to the Futurist rooms at the 1940 Venice Biennale, 'Gli aeropittori e l'aeroritratto simultaneo', in *XXIIᵃ Esposizione Biennale Internazionale d'Arte – 1940-XVIII. Catalogo*, exh. cat., 2ⁿᵈ edn (Venice: Carlo Ferrari, 1940), pp. 181-85 (p. 184).

3     Among others, F. T. Marinetti's iconic 'free-word' poem *Zang Tumb Tumb* (1914). For a full list of titles, see Domenico Cammarota, *Filippo Tommaso Marinetti. Bibliografia* (Milan: Skira; Rovereto: MART, 2002), pp. 161-70.

4     Never before reprinted in full, extracts from *Bombarded Naples Sings* have appeared in surveys such as Vittorio Cappelli's *Futurismo calabrese. Poesie, tavole parolibere, sintesi teatrali* (Soveria Mannelli: Rubbettino, 1997) and Willard Bohn's indispensable volume *Italian Futurist Poetry* (Toronto, Buffalo and New York: University of Toronto Press, 2005).

5     Claudia Salaris, *Storia del futurismo. Libri giornali manifesti*, 2ⁿᵈ rev. edn (Rome: Riuniti, 1992), p. 272.

6     'Caro Busnardo', in Bellanova, *Bombardata Napoli canta*, cit., p. 101; see below, p. 92.

7     Willard Bohn, 'Introduction', in Bohn, *Italian Futurist Poetry*, cit., pp. 3-10 (p. 9).

8     Richard Humphreys, *Futurism* (London: Tate Gallery, 1999), p. 76.

9     Futurism has perhaps the most precisely defined lifespan of any artistic movement. It was officially 'born' on 20 February 1909 with the publication of Marinetti's founding manifesto on the front page of *Le Figaro*, and 'died' with its leader on 2 December 1944.

10    See, for example, Enrico Crispolti, 'Second Futurism', in Emily Braun, ed., *Italian Art in the 20ᵗʰ Century: Painting and Sculpture 1900-1988*, exh. cat. (Munich: Prestel, 1989), pp. 165-71; Enrico Crispolti, 'Svolgimenti del futurismo', in *Gli anni trenta. Arte e cultura in Italia*, exh. cat., 2ⁿᵈ rev. edn (Milan: Mazzotta, 1983), pp. 175-84; Giovanni Lista, *Futurism* (Paris: Terrail, 2001). 'Second Futurism' is an umbrella term that does not delimit a precise period of time, but which is broadly used to denote developments within the movement during the inter-war years and (nominally) those of World War Two. The movement's first, 'heroic', phase has traditionally been seen as having ended after Italy entered the Great War in 1915, with the subsequent deaths of Umberto Boccioni and Antonio Sant'Elia, and the gradual withdrawal of other key figures such as Carlo Carrà and Gino Severini.

11 Matteo D'Ambrosio has noted that during this period "the Futurist movement no longer counted hundreds of members as it had done during the first half of the Thirties". 'Marinetti al fronte russo', in Matteo D'Ambrosio, *Futurismo e altre avanguardie* (Naples: Liguori, 1999), pp. 39-69 (p. 39, n. 4).

12 Günter Berghaus, *Futurism and Politics: Between Anarchist Rebellion and Fascist Reaction, 1909-1944* (Providence and Oxford: Berghahn, 1996), p. 234.

13 Following an initial period of cooperation, Marinetti distanced Futurism from Fascism in 1920 when Mussolini's movement lurched to the right in response to the previous year's disastrous election results. However, Mussolini's subsequent rise to power soon convinced Marinetti of the wisdom of a *rapprochement*. A history of the relationship between Futurism and Fascism is outside the scope of this Introduction, and has moreover been chronicled in depth in a number of dedicated studies, of which Berghaus's *Futurism and Politics* (cit.) is among the most thorough. A useful summary can also be found in Caroline Tisdall and Angelo Bozzolla, *Futurism* (London: Thames and Hudson, 1977), pp. 200-09.

14 Berghaus, *Futurism and Politics*, cit., p. 256.

15 'Avant-Garde and Kitsch', in Charles Harrison and Paul Wood, eds, *Art in Theory 1900-1990: An Anthology of Changing Ideas* (Oxford and Cambridge, MA: Blackwell, 1992), pp. 529-41.

16 For instance, Gianni Eugenio Viola has lamented the manner in which Futurist art "degenerated" into a jarringly conservative "neo-figurative style" during these years. See his *Filippo Tommaso Marinetti: lo spettacolo dell'arte* (Palermo: L'Epos, 2004), p. 156. 'Aeropainting' dominated Futurist art throughout the 1930s. A more militarized variant developed around the middle of the decade in response to Italy's invasion of Ethiopia and intervention in the Spanish Civil War. During World War Two such imagery was defined as *aeropittura di guerra*; for a consideration of the evolution of this latter sub-genre, see my essay 'L'aeropittura di guerra futurista. Un'altra prospettiva', in Maria Giuseppina Di Monte, Giuliana Pieri and Simona Storchi, eds, *Visualizzare la guerra. L'iconografia del conflitto e l'Italia* (Milan and Udine: Mimesis, 2016), pp. 81-98.

17 In addition to Guttuso, painters associated with Corrente included Renato Birolli, Bruno Cassinari, Giuseppe Migneco and Emilio Vedova. Adopting a robust figurative style, the group eschewed "the evasiveness of both pure formalism and mere naturalistic representation". See Pia Vivarelli, 'Personalities and Styles in Figurative Art of the Thirties', in Braun, *Italian Art in the 20th Century*, cit., pp. 181-86 (p. 185). Despite its increasing antagonism toward Fascism, Corrente found favour at the high-profile Premio Bergamo exhibitions during the war years, where Guttuso was awarded prizes in 1940 and 1942 for his politically-charged images *Flight from Etna* and *Crucifixion*.

18  Crali (1910-2000) joined the Futurist movement in 1929 and went on to become one of the most important and successful practitioners of aeropainting. One of his works is illustrated in *Bombarded Naples Sings* (see below, pp. 15, 58).

19  A painter, graphic designer and scenographer, Prampolini (1894-1956) had been an influential exponent of the various stylistic tendencies explored by Futurism since 1913. Like Crali, he contributed an image to *Bombarded Naples Sings* (see below, p. 54), in addition to designing its original cover (Fig. 3).

20  Enrico Prampolini, 'Premessa', in *Mostra del pittore Enrico Prampolini*, exh. cat. (Rome: Galleria di Roma, 1941), pp. 11-14 (p. 12).

21  On the relationship between Futurist painters and abstract artists during these later years, see Elena Di Raddo, '"Una centrale elettrica di imperiosa spiritualità": Marinetti, Ciliberti, Sartoris e gli astratti comaschi', in *Arte Lombarda*, June 2011, pp. 109-22.

22  *The Other Modernism: F. T. Marinetti's Futurist Fiction of Power* (Berkeley, Los Angeles and London: University of California Press, 1996), p. 146.

23  Marinetti set out the principles of aeropoetry in a manifesto of 1931 titled 'L'aeropoesia. Manifesto futurista ai poeti e agli aviatori'. On the theory and development of this style, see Willard Bohn, 'The Poetics of Flight: Futurist "Aeropoesia"', in *MLN*, vol. 121, no. 1, January 2006, pp. 207-24.

24  See, for example, Bruno Aschieri, *L'aeropoema futurista dei legionari in Spagna* (Rome: Edizioni Futuriste di 'Poesia', 1941), Ennio De Concini, *Aeropoesie futuriste di bombardamenti* (Rome: Edizioni Futuriste di 'Poesia', 1941), F. T. Marinetti, *Canto eroi e macchine della guerra mussoliniana* (Milan and Verona: Mondadori, 1942), and the anthologies *Carlinga di aeropoeti futuristi di guerra* (Rome: Mediterraneo Futurista, [1941]) and *Ad Amedeo Savoia Aosta. Omaggio di aeropoesie guerriere offerto dagli aeropoeti futuristi* (Rome: Edizioni Futuriste di 'Poesia', 1942).

25  F. T. Marinetti, 'Destruction of Syntax – Imagination without Strings – Words-in-Freedom', in Umbro Apollonio, ed., *Futurist Manifestos* (Boston: MFA, 2001), pp. 95-106 (pp. 104-05). The relatively conventional typographical character of aeropoetry was, in part, a consequence of the fact that it was intended to be heard rather than seen: "Aeropoems find their natural vehicle in the Radio" (this citation is taken from the version of Marinetti's aforementioned text 'L'aeropoesia. Manifesto futurista ai poeti e agli aviatori' published under the same title in *Futurismo* on 2 October 1932; repr. in Luciano Caruso, ed., *Manifesti, proclami, interventi e documenti teorici del futurismo 1909-1944*, 4 vols (Florence: SPES-Salimbeni, 1980), vol. II, no. 218).

26  'Words more-or-less in freedom': a description used by the critic Giacomo Debenedetti in writing of one of Marinetti's late works. 'Il *Poema africano* di Marinetti', in Giacomo Debenedetti, *Saggi critici. Seconda serie* (Milan: Il

Saggiatore, 1971), pp. 225-33 (p. 226).

27 Sartini Blum, *The Other Modernism*, cit., p. 146.

28 Marinetti, 'Destruction of Syntax', cit., p. 98.

29 Ibid., p. 106. See, for example, De Concini's use of verbal distortion and onomatopoeia in his poem 'Bombardamento di Londra' (*Aeropoesie futuriste di bombardamenti*, cit., pp. 23-26). Bellanova's elongation of the word 'echo' in the present text is another instance of this ('Alla donna dei combattenti', pp. 33-36 (p. 33); see below, pp. 50-52 (p. 50)).

30 In these respects, one of the worst offenders was Ignazio Scurto. See his poems 'Uno squadrista moriva' and 'Poema dell'impero' in the aforementioned anthology *Carlinga di aeropoeti futuristi di guerra*, pp. 64-70.

31 Mary Ellen Solt, ed., *Concrete Poetry: A World View* (Bloomington and London: Indiana University Press, 1968), p. 37.

32 Carlo Belloli, 'Poesia visuale', in Carlo Belloli, *Testi-Poemi murali* (Milan: ERRE, 1944), p. 5.

33 Ibid.

34 Tullio Crali and F. T. Marinetti, *Parole musicali – Alfabeto in libertà. Manifesto futurista* (Venice: Movimento Futurista Italiano, 1944).

35 According to Crali and Marinetti, "Musical words [...] will find understanding and integration within any nation of any people of any tongue, as with any other musical work. The title will be the sole guide, and will be sufficient to eliminate any misunderstandings deriving from racial and cultural differences." *Parole musicali*, cit. Given that this manifesto was written within the borders of Mussolini's Italian Social Republic – nothing more than a puppet state of Hitler's regime, directly controlled by the SS – it strikes a remarkably progressive note in its proposal of a poetic theory celebrating diversity rather than division, endorsing internationalism rather than nationalism, and proclaiming the expressive power of 'primitivism' to be superior to the artistic achievements of Western civilization. Viewed in this context, the manifesto may even bear interpretation as a repudiation of the cultural isolationism and racism of Nazi-Fascism.

36 Crali and Marinetti, *Parole musicali*, cit.

37 See Vladimir Markov, *Russian Futurism: A History* (London: MacGibbon & Kee, 1969).

38 Enrico Prampolini, *Arte polimaterica (verso un'arte collettiva?)* (Rome: OET – Edizioni del Secolo, 1944), p. 14; original emphasis.

39 F . T. Marinetti, 'Collaudo i "Testi-Poemi murali" di Carlo Belloli', in Belloli, *Testi-Poemi murali*, cit., p. 3.

40 'Aeropoema-collaudo scritto dal poeta F. T. Marinetti', cit., p. 18; see below, p. 40. The volume's original cover also defined it as an *aeropoema futurista*.

41    Umbro Apollonio, 'I firmatari del primo manifesto futurista', in *XXV Biennale di Venezia. Catalogo*, exh. cat. (Venice: Alfieri, 1950), pp. 55-58 (p. 55).

42    A view ascribed to Crali by Claudio Rebeschini. See his 'Prefazione' in Mirella Duci, ed., *Fondo Tullio Crali. Inventario* (Rovereto: Nicolodi; MART, 2008), pp. 11-13 (p. 11).

43    Scrivo (1901-1976) collaborated with Bellanova on various Futurist initiatives during the 1940s (see below) and was also Marinetti's personal secretary from shortly after the end of the First World War until Futurism's dissolution in 1944. During the 1930s he established the ALA (Agenzia Letteraria Artistica) press agency to promote Futurist activity. This reflected the fact that articles and statements in newspapers – rather than privately printed leaflets and manifestos – had by that point become the movement's preferred vehicles for the communication of its ideas. See Salaris, *Storia del futurismo*, cit., pp. 199-200.

44    'Rapporti Mario Menin-Futurismo', in Luigi Scrivo, *Mario Menin Camicia Nera Futurista e primo battaglista del mondo* (Rome: Edizioni Futuriste di 'Poesia', 1941), pp. 13-16 (pp. 14-15); original emphasis (*liberissimamente*).

45    F. T. Marinetti, Emilio Settimelli and Mario Carli, 'Che cos'è il futurismo. Nozioni elementari'; repr. in Caruso, *Manifesti*, cit., vol. II, no. 137.

46    Founded in 1923, the Consiglio Nazionale delle Ricerche (CNR) is Italy's largest public research institute.

47    Although primarily a political journal, *Calabria Fascista* (1922-42) frequently featured articles on Futurism during the 1930s. Those contributed by Bellanova were: 'Tradizione e modernolatria' (14 August 1937), 'Marinetti e il Futurismo' (8 August 1938) and 'Fascismo – Futurismo – Arditismo' (28 August 1938).

48    'Il romanzo sintetico. Manifesto futurista', in *Il Giornale d'Italia*, 24 December 1939; repr. in Caruso, *Manifesti*, cit., vol. III, no. 297.

49    F. T. Marinetti, Emilio Settimelli and Bruno Corra, 'The Futurist Synthetic Theatre' (1915), in Apollonio, *Futurist Manifestos*, cit., pp. 183-96 (p. 193); original emphasis.

50    *Picchiata nell'amore* (Rome: Unione Editoriale d'Italia, 1940). In addition to reprinting the manifesto 'Il romanzo sintetico', the volume featured two effusive introductory texts by Scrivo and Marinetti; the latter was appropriately concise, stretching to just five short paragraphs.

51    The other was Geppo Tedeschi's *Gli Adoratori della Patria* (Lanciano: Carabba, 1941).

52    Held in Rome between 18 November 1938 and 9 May 1939, the *Mostra autarchica minerale italiano* was a propaganda exercise with pronounced Modernist overtones, incorporating three-dimensional murals and installations by Prampolini.

53    Marinetti, Scrivo and Bellanova, 'Il romanzo sintetico', cit.; original emphasis.

It is not known which of the ideas contained in the manifesto were contributed by Bellanova; however, this particular point may represent an early expression of his interest in the cinema (see below, p. 13).

54  Marinetti, Scrivo and Bellanova, 'Il romanzo sintetico', cit.

55  *Picchiata nell'amore*, cit., p. 29.

56  The review featured on p. 60 of the September 1940 edition of Gio Ponti's journal.

57  On this exhibition, see Anna Caterina Toni, *Futuristi nelle Marche* (Rome: De Luca, 1982), pp. 96-97.

58  An account of this episode, which took place on 22 January 1941, can be found in Günter Berghaus, *Italian Futurist Theatre 1909-1944* (Oxford: Clarendon Press, 1998), p. 547. See also Mario Verdone, 'Memoria su Piero Bellanova e "La piccola città" di Thornton Wilder', in Mario Verdone, *Drammaturgia e arte totale. L'avanguardia internazionale – Autori, teorie, opere*, ed. by Rocco Mario Morano (Soveria Mannelli: Rubbettino, 2005), pp. 71-78. According to Marinetti, the dramatist Luigi Bonelli (1892-1954) was also involved in the protest; see his text 'Tumultuosa serata al Teatro Argentina di Roma in difesa del primato teatrale italiano', in F. T. Marinetti, *Il teatro futurista* (Naples: CLET, 1941), pp. 3-4 (p. 3).

59  Berghaus, *Italian Futurist Theatre*, cit., p. 547.

60  Marinetti, 'Tumultuosa serata al Teatro Argentina', cit., pp. 3, 4. Punctuation was largely absent from later Futurist texts, in accordance with the principles of aeropoetry (as the poet Pino Masnata wryly observed in an article of 1935, "in an aeroplane it is not possible to stop in the sky"). 'Parole in libertà e distruzione della punteggiatura', in *Stile Futurista*, vol. 2, nos 11-12, September 1935, pp. 38-39 (p. 38). Bellanova adheres to this convention throughout *Bombarded Naples Sings*.

61  For a detailed history of this institution, see Roberto Di Ferdinando's article 'La Scuola di Sanità Militare nel Chiostro del Maglio' at: http://curiositadifirenze.blogspot.co.uk/2011/04/la-scuola-di-sanita-militare-nel.html [accessed 7 February 2017].

62  F. T. Marinetti, Luigi Scrivo and Piero Bellanova, 'L'arte tipografica di guerra e dopoguerra. Manifesto futurista', in *Graphicus*, no. 5, May 1942 (the version cited here is that repr. in Caruso, *Manifesti*, cit., vol. III, no. 298, which also lists Alfredo Trimarco as a signatory of the text).

63  F. T. Marinetti, Farfa, Giovanni Acquaviva and Aldo Giuntini, eds, *Canzoniere futurista amoroso guerriero* (Savona: Istituto Grafico Brizio, 1943). For instance, Gaetano Pattarozzi's 'song' 'Volando sulla Sardegna' was in fact an awkwardly de-contextualized excerpt from his *Aeropoema futurista della Sardegna* (Rome: Edizioni Futuriste di 'Poesia', [1939]).

64 F. T. Marinetti, Farfa, Giovanni Acquaviva, Aldo Giuntini and Luigi Scrivo, 'Collaudo di Marinetti Farfa Acquaviva Giuntini Scrivo. Canzoni passate passatiste futuriste', in Marinetti, and others, *Canzoniere futurista amoroso guerriero*, cit., n. p.

65 See F. T. Marinetti, 'La poesia mobilitata a servizio della guerra', in *Autori e Scrittori*, February 1943, p. 2 (Cra.3.17).

66 Ibid.

67 See 'Il 2° dinamismo di poesie guerriere del Sindacato Autori e Scrittori', in *Il Lavoro fascista*, 27 May 1943 (Cra.3.32). The first *dinamismo* had taken place earlier that month, on 8 May.

68 See 'Il 2° dinamismo di poesie guerriere', in *Il Popolo di Trieste*, 6 June 1943 (Cra.3.33). According to this review, Bellanova read 'Bombarded Naples Sings' and 'The Soldier's Woman' – the latter presumably corresponding to the poem titled 'To the Soldiers' Woman' in the present volume. Bellanova's book was previewed again at the third *dinamismo* on 25 June.

69 *Volgarizzazione del Futurismo. Ideologie – Storia – Sviluppi – Chiarificazioni sul movimento futurista italiano e mondiale*. This volume appears to have had a rather extended period of gestation, having already been announced three years earlier in *Nose-diving into Love*. It is not known what became of either this project or Bellanova's novel *Il Grande futuro*.

70 A number of poems dating from the period 1942-46 were later gathered together by Bellanova in an anthology of 1977. A second edition of this text was published in more recent years: *Ascoltare le stelle* (Cosenza: CJC, 2011).

71 Cra.3.251.

72 Tullio Crali, 'Una vita per il Futurismo. Tra scossoni e vuoti d'aria alla ricerca di quota', in Claudio Rebeschini, ed., *Crali aeropittore futurista*, exh. cat. (Milan: Electa, 1994), pp. 143-267 (p. 205).

73 This was the case with Prampolini, who enthusiastically promoted the work of the Forma group of abstract painters in his capacity as Vice President of the Art Club, founded in Rome in 1945. Farfa (Vittorio Osvaldo Tommasini) also successfully adapted to the post-war status quo; the playful and absurdist spirit that had characterized his Futurist work was championed by Enrico Baj during the 1950s, and he participated in the activities of the latter's Movimento nucleare.

74 On Benedetta, see below, pp. 77-78.

75 Crali, 'Una vita per il Futurismo', cit., p. 185.

76 See, for instance, his correspondence with Crali dating from the late 1970s and early 1980s (Cra.10.66, Cra.10.203, Cra.10.220 and Cra.10.237).

77 On the Ministero per la Costituente (1945-46), see http://search.acs. beniculturali.it/OpacACS/guida/IT-ACS-AS0001-0000614 [accessed 16

March 2017].

78 Like Bellanova, Servadio (1904-1995) was a poet and a man of culture. His interest in conventional psychology was paralleled by a fascination with paranormal phenomena, such as telepathy.

79 'Prefazione', in Gianna Giuliani, *Le strisce interiori. Cinema italiano e psicoanalisi* (Rome: Bulzoni, 1980), pp. 5-11.

80 Secretary (1969-86); Vice President (1986-87).

81 See Luisa Corda's brief overview of Bellanova's contribution to psychoanalysis at: http://www.spiweb.it/elenco-voci-spipedia/7034-bellanova-piero [accessed 2 February 2017].

82 *Naples '44: An Intelligence Officer in the Italian Labyrinth* (London: Eland, 2002).

83 On the Allies' bombing campaign in Italy during the Second World War, see Claudia Baldoli, 'I bombardamenti sull'Italia nella Seconda Guerra Mondiale. Strategia anglo-americana e propaganda rivolta alla popolazione civile', in *DEP – Deportate, esuli, profughe*, nos 13-14, 2010, pp. 34-49.

84 Letter of 16 August 1941 (Cra.2.207).

85 Ibid.

86 See below, p. 58.

87 The earliest of these is dated April 1942 ('Caro Buccafusca', p. 91; see below, p. 87); the latest is dated August 1943, the month of the text's publication ('Caro Busnardo', cit.).

88 The dates of these 'letters' do not necessarily correspond to the dates of the poems themselves; accordingly, they do not disprove the hypothesis that at least some of the compositions included in *Bombarded Naples Sings* had been completed by August 1941.

89 As we have seen, Bellanova did occasionally participate in public recitals during the war years.

90 Wherever it has been possible to discover biographical information regarding the figures to whom Bellanova's 'letters' are addressed, this has been provided in the notes to the text.

91 See the entry on this manifesto in Cammarota, *Filippo Tommaso Marinetti*, cit., p. 140 / 90. The version cited here is that published as 'Manifesto futurista dell'amicizia di guerra' in *Il Giornale d'Italia* on 12 February 1942; repr. in Caruso, *Manifesti*, cit., vol. III, no. 313.

92 Marinetti and Cangiullo, 'Manifesto futurista dell'amicizia di guerra', cit. Two volumes of letters exchanged by the authors of this manifesto were also compiled by Cangiullo during these years. One of them related to Marinetti's participation in the Ethiopian campaign of the mid-1930s, the other comprised correspondence dating from the Futurist leader's period of military service in the Soviet Union in 1942 (see below, p. 103, n. 52). *Lettere a Marinetti in Africa*

(Naples: Tommaso Pironti, 1940); *DON Napoli* (Naples: CLET, 1943).

93    Salaris, *Storia del futurismo*, cit., p. 278.

94    First published as 'Manifesto futurista. Nuova estetica della guerra' in *Il Giornale d'Italia* on 20 September 1940. According to Duci (*Fondo Tullio Crali*, cit., p. 101), the version cited here – 'Nuova estetica della guerra' (Cra.2.141) – appeared in the same journal between September and October 1940, although the document itself is not clear on this point.

95    'Collaudo fatto da F. T. Marinetti Accademico d'Italia', in Eugenio Caracciolo, *Il poema del tecnicismo del Basso Sulcis* (Rome: Edizioni Futuriste di 'Poesia', 1941), pp. 5-6 (p. 5).

96    'L'aerosilurante', pp. 39-41 (p. 39); see below, pp. 55-56 (p. 55).

97    On this subject, see Joshua S. Goldstein, *War and Gender: How Gender Shapes the War System and Vice Versa* (Cambridge: Cambridge University Press, 2003), pp. 338-39.

98    F. T. Marinetti, *Come si seducono le donne e si tradiscono gli uomini* (Milan: Sonzogno, [1920]), p. 72.

99    Ibid., p. 64.

100   See Giordano Bruno Guerri, *Filippo Tommaso Marinetti. Invenzioni, avventure e passioni di un rivoluzionario* (Milan: Mondadori, 2010), p. 257. On Marinetti's membership of the Reale Accademia d'Italia, see below, p. 98, n. 1.

101   'L'amore sintetico mediterraneo', in *Autori e Scrittori*, September 1941; repr. in Caruso, *Manifesti*, cit., vol. III, no. 309.

102   Marinetti, and others, 'Collaudo di Marinetti Farfa Acquaviva Giuntini Scrivo', cit., n. p.

103   'Alla donna dei combattenti', cit., pp. 34-35; see below, p. 51.

104   'Volare su Venezia', pp. 73-75 (p. 73); see below, pp. 75-76 (p. 75).

105   Humphreys, *Futurism*, cit., p. 76.

# BOMBARDED NAPLES SINGS

# Contents

# Aeropoem-inspection[2]
# written by the Poet
# F. T. Marinetti

Since many people envy Naples to the extent that they bombard her with explosive devices it is necessary to enumerate not only the anti-aircraft batteries but also the arms and munitions of poetry of sentiment of passion and You aeropoets ready to sing these simultaneous harmonies of words in freedom

You are as inviting as a clam brimming with liquid sky o beautiful terrace by the sea and I anticipate your eager coterie all pepper lemons laughter of young Neapolitan women crowding together to listen to a letter from the poet Buccafusca[3] serving at the Russian front

"I am writing this letter to you from Gomel where I have come to escape the serene calm of Kolomea and to satisfy my desire to live the bellicose dynamic life that you Marinetti have celebrated constantly throughout the first half of this century[4]

War which is impossible to fight without love has conquered me despite the love of Angelina

You will understand what I mean by the sentimental baggage of those who implore you to remain when you are on the point of departing who beg you to return quickly while you patiently await the moment to enjoy a taste of glory

The batteries' searchlights seem like the long mobile fingers of the frozen earth that wants to pull the sky's starry blanket down over itself

The city walls support the roof of the sky sheltering twisted metalwork and piles of rubble amidst rigid blazings velveted with lampblack empty eye sockets of Cubist women that no artist will ever paint again

You are constantly in my thoughts and my memories my great *Marinettissimo*[5] prodigious animator tireless immense creator"

O how they kiss and try to embrace one another those young and old houses facades courtyards colours of Casciaro[6] and communicating vases of flowers pink dark blue jealousy and optimism beneath towering balconies of Damocles

Who will be able to cork the sparkling passion of the alleyways of compressed love conduits for frenzied pressings?

Those climbing serenades will cling to Coma Berenices[7] having their roots in the soft soil of a little boat infused with sea moon and geraniums drunk on the Gregale[8] and the cricked neck of lost love

I challenge anyone to halt the impetuous joyful sadness of this formation of mandolins marching to rhythmical slashes in the flesh of melancholy

They cut the silence and force it to reach up to arouse the most frigid star

Aeropoets let's drink a good cup of Italian pride before the long long *lagrime*[9] of guitars in fish taverns skimming the water become daggers in the barbed wire of love that heartens a reinforcement of a hundred *scugnizzi*[10] Rinaldos Clorindas Suleimans[11] with their *putipùs scetavaiasses tofas*[12] etc.

I have no time to groom myself and race off to the Giardino degli Aranci all of Posillipo being an atomizer of acacia bergamot mandarin roses and without me it finally sensualizes the fluttering linen of Mediterranean ports

Dressed in lilac Vesuvius smokes elegantly wearily baring her sides[13] or dressed in her finery up up to a black *bautta*[14] from behind which a vermillion glance blazes

The mermaids are defeated defeated in their legendary beauty if they leap into the deep blue shining salty rowers geometries of oars muscles with fugitive emerald reflections generated by Benedetta's indigo speeds flashing with gold[15]

Look down there they are exciting the siesta of Prampolini's Capri bather[16] as she enjoys the grotto's fluid crystal above and below foam amongst lapis lazuli twittering to the whispers risks hissings of the seabirds flying away

One day I will be able to dream on those docile box-seats full of joyful ballistite[17] in the afternoon's Villa if a dalliance of camerus with bamboo palms protects it with aromatic shadows

The most suspicious of policemen must turn a blind eye to the innumerable conspiratorial whispers of the little waves on the surface of Mergellina's streets especially now that they are guzzled by a jealous subterranean hollow

But the sun-charged cobblestones burn the blue water with kisses and marry it murmuring you will be mine and we will have two beautiful little tykes who we will take for walks to the slow rhythms of the Sirocco

Oof how can one digest the weight of the afternoon after lunching on pasta with pettifogging quibbles in sauce and the blood of infidelity exasperated by the desire to remain faithful

Lament lament I know that in reality you are happy o beautiful mothers seated in nostalgic armchairs on the large balcony and so navigate your way across the sky toward a seraphic adultery o you who are as faithful as oysters deep down

Every originality every caprice with Panama hats boaters monocles walking-sticks gardenias in buttonholes they visit discuss approve the rooms of poets and painters on balconies overlooking the Gulf and down below the supplementary permanently open exhibition of the street rejoices

Let's dine in this high restaurant overhanging the jumble of houses cottages villas and damp abysses where far below fish flash almost frying dreaming of leaping into one's mouth if all of a sudden the traffic warden Love intones the round *do*[18] of its full moon like a tenor

Suddenly denuded by the music the lovers adjourn what agony those 29 urgent kisses

I too have risen and proceed on elastic legs convinced that at this moment the dwarfs of Toledo are also toasting the inebriated glass of heavy frames with their foreheads

No other city in the world can boast of such ostentatious elegance with warm fresh beautiful women on divans and at flowered railings

They are lavishly envied by gardens of roses kept as prisoners or escaping through gates like lovers if the news vendor shrieks *Mattino Roma Corriere di Napoli* menacing fan of the latest events

Communism's immense dust cloud of baked mud soars overhead to massacre everyone from on high

But against it is hurled the festival of S. Lucia with its spectacular sailing ship of fireworks[19]

This is carried along on the shoulders of 38 youths

It is constructed and destroyed by the hands of the pyrotechnicians who consol it with the pitch of the sobbing and saliva of much-kissed babies

Although enormous it will fit through the doors

The church of S. Lucia a Mare[20] has become a vast porcupine of lit lamps each one merrily competing with the sun's rays

— Set off firecrackers Catherine-wheels all the way to the legs of the priests dripping with gold and silver and the babies laugh clinging to breasts as if to buoys

Unfortunately a waaawailing abruptly bursts forth the drill-like roaring of the bombers grinders of sharp money they are coming they are coming the balmy air is corrupted by it and rockets of mocking fantasy whistle with stems lilies showers of adamantine petals

The sweetness of the incense is as tenderly implacable as that of the prayers accompanied by a brimming organ which overflows with tears

It rises up to construct the facade of a new cathedral-like Naples with spirals of children's voices and with gravid cupolas and bell-clappers that dance the most beautiful Sundays on earth

On the pinnacle stands the purest Immaculate Madonna with a thousand halos and S. Gennaro[21] in shining brass with a thousand crucifixes in his glittering right hand

— Undress undress boys or you will burn with so many thunderbolts on your heads

— We instead are men caparisoned like the horses that gallop back wildly from the festival of the Divine Love diving in fully clothed

Even the tablecloths dressed up to the nines in their glasses and dishes are mesmerized by the swarthy buxom water vendors

They smile like fruits with fussy little teeth beneath arches resplendent with yellow lemons and lit oil lamps venerating the Sacred Heart of Jesus

An ebony seaquake of hair and vast liquorice eyes writhes about while the mouth kisses and nourishes the air resounding with *italianità*[22] and the joy of living

The air is a luxurious window display of a shop owned by everyone since each product can be bought and eaten and the beautiful street carries the passers-by along on their ever faster faster course

Just as swiftly it is necessary to praise these breasts tactilisms[23] of blossoming snow-white silk that cultivate gardens for bracelets languid looks and in order to slake the thirst of the Tyrrhenian ablaze with coral fluid little sparkling clouds of elder in a bellicose ball of mirth

All of a sudden the organ of S. Lucia announces a counter-attack

Bellowing like a bull from its deep bamboo thickets the organ reproaches the excessive sweetness of the childlike voices and informs all the cannons of the lofty batteries that it will help them

Encouraged the cannons immediately take control

In the breathless thronging of their vehement mouths metallic elbows of flame stab one another and since it is necessary necessary quickly to hurl precisely measured lumps of lead up to the heavens calculate shoot calculate shoot

Evacuate I insist evacuate up there large boxes of poisoned biscuits

Yes yes you are hit and split rolled packaged you will plummet filled with lead like smoking cigars from the bellies of bankers

But down down flexuously caressing the laziness of Capri and Ischia although they do not deem you worthy of a bitter perfume damned bombers

Liquidated

— I Gaspare Molo Beverello of Italian Literature son of Casella the Deaf[24] pontiff of books captain of literary barges and friend of Anatole France[25] affirm it

Sirens sound the all-clear with a Vesuvian olfactory tactilism of tar fennel ashes and watermelons accompanied by wheels thundering over the cobblestones

A tattered peanut vendor with a tray around his neck

— Buy a *spasso*[26] now that death has passed by

— It passed by tragically given that so many holy churches have been destroyed and that so many mothers with their offspring lie crushed beneath the ground

Thereupon appears the caracoling miracle that has already routed every evil influence

Radiant fragrant fresh she seems more rose than woman gracefully poised on the naked back of a black colt

Alongside a tricolour carnation balances on the naked back of a snow-white horse running with 20 legs painted by Boccioni Futurist ex libris savoured by the lovers of manuscripts Treccani Di Marzio Pariani Bastianini[27]

Gladdening the air the breath of Lombardy's lakes awakens books from their sensual torpor stupor flapping in the marine sunshine like seagulls

*Air of Capri* by Cerio and *Astra and the Submarine* by Benedetta *Piedigrotta Café Concert Synthetic Theatre Poetry in Pentagrams Futurist Evenings* by Francesco Cangiullo *Essence of Futurism* by Acquaviva

*French Poems* by Libero Russo *The Aeropoem of Sardinia* by Pattarozzi and *Optimism at Any Cost* by Sanzin *Mother Air* by Civello *When I was a Shepherd* by Giardina *Airport* by Scurto *Short Circuits* by Geppo Tedeschi *The Bull* by Bruno Corra *Poetry of Surgical Instruments* by Pino Masnata[28]

A merry tactilism of pages that share confidences each one speaking to the other from its heart

A highly attentive single female reader bends down from the zenith the ultra-Neapolitan Pole Star

She begins to read *Bombarded Naples Sings* by Piero Bellanova the continuation of his celebrated Futurist synthetic novel *Nose-diving into Love*[29]

Floating in a cloak dating from the days of the giants the immortal *scugnizzo* attempts to roll up his sleeves and show his nerve but prefers astronomically to direct the entire quarter of Piazza dei Francesi with his megaphone of pink cardboard

— In Bellanova's book it is written that if they hit the centre of Piazza Municipio I must also be at the centre

Listen everyone Piero Bellanova trained himself by composing the Manifesto of the Synthetic Novel with Marinetti and Luigi Scrivo[30]

Highly accomplished and with stupefying intensity and variety he sings the drama of our Naples the most colourful and musical of all cities yet ready to pounce with supercilious feline fury

Laud the words in freedom of the already illustrious young aeropoet Piero Bellanova who knows better than other writers how to

1) Express the modern acceleration of carnal and sentimental love
2) Synthesize the ideal woman of the young male Futurist
3) Fuse woman with machine
4) Perfect a fusion of woman + machine + war

And the prodigy of this fusion emerges in the Futurist aeropainting of

Gerardo Dottori who having plastically bound blossoming Umbrian almond trees with Umbrian breasts has now mixed a tremendous and machine-gunning aerial battle with these somnolent hearts and blessed seas of ours[31]

Piero Bellanova's *Bombarded Naples Sings* has such dynamism that it can serve as an auxiliary engine or parachute if one takes it into the fuselage

On the threshold of Casella's bookshop the immortal *scugnizzo* proclaims

— I guarantee its speciaaal originality

Chiurazzi who cast Boccioni's *Speeding Muscles*[32] Mannaiolo Comisso Giusso the poet Barbieri Chuzeville Palazzeschi[33] all enter with sinuous swaggering gaits

Learned and exquisite clandestine meeting coming and going in front of Placido

The Futurists Cangiullo Buccafusca Bellanova Tedeschi Scrivo Pattarozzi Giardina Civello brusquely appear gathering around Gaspare Casella with copies of *Bombarded Naples Sings* in their hands

Siniscalchi Tecchio Milone Toffanin Carafa Assante Carlo Barbieri Sansanelli Foschini Corona suddenly arrive[34]

The rowdiest of discussions

— Is the subject indispensable in painting?

— Is it indispensable for a poet to participate in the life of the Fatherland and to celebrate its deeds?

— Are the lessons in absolute patriotism at the National Gallery of Futurist Art indispensable? [35]

The Futurists peremptorily respond yes

The cultural xenomanes twist and turn evasively

Casella responds to Chuzeville who sighs over the victories of the Futurists

— Bu[36] do you remember when we woke Marinetti up in Paris with our sing-song in the corridor of the Hôtel Lutetia[37]

> ' na casarella
> pittata 'e rose
> ncoppa e Camaldule
> vurria pe' te[38]

and when he awoke Marinetti showed us this journal *Les Marges* which is forthright on the subject of Futurist originality being plagiarized abroad

I translate

"Mallarmé is the grandfather of the former Dadaist Surrealists Aragon and Breton.[39] Marinetti is their father. They have stolen everything from Marinetti: trousers, socks, nervous tics.

Marinetti thundered incendiary manifestos; so did they.

Marinetti emulated Rabelais;[40] so did they.

Marinetti abused *le mot de Cambronne*;[41] so did they.

Futurist words in freedom were the first manifestations of the Dadaist spirit and I challenge anyone to deny it.

Marinetti defended the role of the unconscious in poetry; so did they. Had they too gone to war it would have been impossible to distinguish them from their father.

Signed by the renowned French poet Louis Mandin."[42]

Having become drowsy guitars and mandolins embrace one another in sleep like puppies and kittens in the houses' fearless orchard

The sunset which never laughs in literature washes the Castel dell'Ovo[43] with the most delicious velvety tones of Veronese greenpink flesh[44]

The Neapolitan night becomes a deep blue reading room with lamps to study by

Greedy for downed enemy bombers the infinite darkness awaits foresees the next alarm

F. T. MARINETTI
Futurist aeropoet

*To Italy's mutilated cities
and the innumerable Italian heroes
of land sea sky*

# Dear Guadagnini

On that evening in November 1942 when us old friends from the Medical Officer Training Course said goodbye to one another in Florence[45] shattering the combined solidity of our hearts in order to scatter the splinters across the war's various fronts I said

"Our soul has a white uniform and a red cross that flashes with faith and with love for a beautiful woman to whom we have all been devoted and who we will now finally be able to kiss with lips turned to steel

This woman is Italy who others wish to possess

Marinetti writes to me from Russia using a phrase that will become our motto ADORE ITALY"[46]

Today you write to me from your Sardinian field hospital describing how long steel tears frequently rain down around you forming rivulets of blood and I experience again the emotion of our embrace that evening while I sing this two-hundredth alarm in Naples

*May 1943*

GERARDO DOTTORI

*Inferno of Aerial Battle above the Paradise of the Gulf*[47]

# Bombarded Naples Sings

Naples you are beautiful
with your heavy blue veil
unable to conceal
the inviting red mouth
of Vesuvius

The crazed sirens howl

The enemy has motorized itself
so as not to be bewitched
by the spells
of a tremulous mandolin whose notes
rain from the stars
on the sweetness of Mergellina

Hurling itself with jealous rage
on the enchanted gulf
that boils cauldrons of lava
mixed with swathes of shadow

From Vomero to Posillipo
flames of hatred blaze

The volcano shakes

Clawing
steely lava
from the bowels of the earth
to hurl against the enemy
which it longs to suffocate
with infinite tresses of smoke[48]

Naples
your blouse
embroidered with rainbow hues
is today spanned by a ruby necklace
of vermillion droplets

It is the blood of your sons
that wants to glorify
your eternal
i n d e s t r u c t i b l e
beauty

# Augusto Platone
# Gold Medal
## Killed in action on Mount Golico[49]

While the dawn shone like nickel on the sorrowful dreams of your woman you impetuously sacrificed your youth on the slopes of Mount Golico as a Futurist aeropoet fortified by three wars for our supreme love Italy

The long blasts of silver trumpets resound with a rhythmic echo of the battalions that accompany your march into glory

Now you rise above the skyscrapers constructed from the songs of bombarded Naples that Sant'Elia[50] erects in your honour as poet of the cityscape and the machine[51]

The stars lower their golden eyes as your light passes

**FUTURIST GOLD MEDAL**

*December 1942*

# To the Soldiers' Woman

You were born from the loud thud
of a hand grenade
that fell close to me
O BEAUTIFUL WOMAN OF MY REVERIES
a fragile blue harmony
in a poem orchestrated by cannons
and the strident violins
of whistling bullets

I see you again after the attack
while cleaning
my dagger's bloodied blade

Your smile is pervaded
by the jealous sneer of the prisoner
filthy with mud

Your crystal voice
is like an eeecho
of the moans of the wounded
in whose blood
a mother's silver tears flow

I adore violence
that shatters the universe

with a single blow
yet I love the languid
sensual caress
of your long hands
as lithe as birch shoots

Your supple and slender waist
is wrapped in the rain of liquefied skies

Your eyes are blue wells
reflecting the long shadows
of your black eyelashes

I savour the harmonious elasticity
of your ankles
while my rough hands
want to break
your fragility
and my parched lips
gather kisses from your mouth
like almond blossom
and fleshy strawberries

I want to wind
a string of dewdrops
around your graceful neck

But listen

The attack begins again

Quickly

Give me your luminous heart

I want to lock it away
in that enemy fort

which I shall conquer for your light
with a dagger between my teeth
with your dream in my soul

I have recorded this song
on a propeller's disc

It will be amplified for you
in the dream's ether
by a trimotor bomber
O AEROWOMAN OF MY REVERIES

# My dear and great Marinetti

The explosion of my Futurist joy reaches you on the Russian steppe where you are fighting your fifth war[52]

Today I am gathering up the sobbing of the Neapolitan people and carrying it to the stars to hurl it away with a roar

It is a static block of iron in space that my torpedo-bomber wants to render dynamic

I have always dreamed of conducting an orchestra of machine-guns torpedoes cannons from a podium of sun

*October 1942*

ENRICO PRAMPOLINI
*The Poet Marinetti at the Russian Front*[53]

# The Torpedo-bomber

An enemy cruiser
swiftly brutally presses
marine waves-breasts
their frothing milk
s c a t t e r i n g
in liquid songs of nostalgia

The torpedo-bomber has pierced
the horizon's grey silk
like a tiny inkblot
on the skysea's damp paper
made for love letters

Now the propeller announces
its noisy presence
to the beautiful steel ship
with a roaring serenade of war

Jealous cannons defend
the naked virginity
of the gleaming bow
with iron blasts

The heedless aircraft
skims the water

At 800 metres
i t  r e l e a s e s
the impatient love token
that races
to press a dusky orchid
crushed by nervous little hands
against the flesh
of the coy beauty

Meanwhile the torpedo-bomber
swoops to steal
the heart of the moribund siren
and departs
burning
in a wake of impalpable atoms
forests lakes sunsets
that release the scent
of Italian earth

The moon undoes its veil
woven from threads of white gold

Suspended in heaven's infinity
it seems a light hammock
rocked by the trembling of the first stars
offering repose
to the aerowarrior

# Dear Ciruzzi

Your Naples sings despite being bombarded

She defends herself with her colours and the great heart of the Neapolitans is an unsheathed and glittering sword that longs to strike

They can destroy everything except the God-given beauty of your Gulf

And in protecting it the aeroplanes become as jealous as your love

*January 1943*

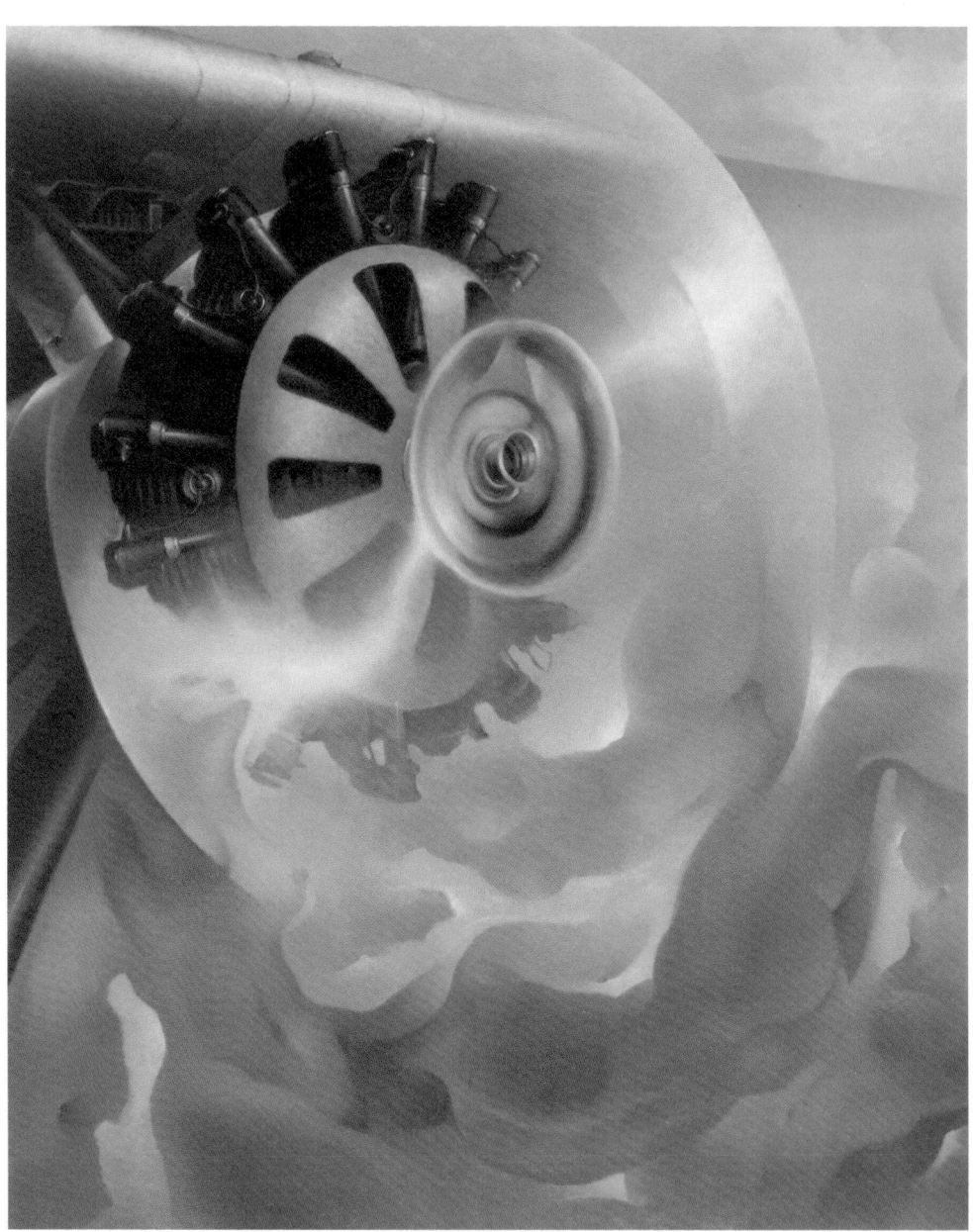

TULLIO CRALI
*Seducer of Clouds*[54]

# Jealousies of Trimotors

From a hangar of green trees
a reckless
off-duty fighter
launches itself into the sky

Acrobatically biting
the sinuous curves
of languid pink clouds
hidden amongst blue veils

Emasculated by dusk
the Sun sadly spurts its last
sanguineous drops
into the sky

Transformed
into the Moon's compliant eunuch
it scatters velvety cushions of flowering wisteria
across the sky's carpet
expediting the passions
of the odalisque clouds
which the fighter boldly penetrates

Erotic saraband
punctuated by glittering stars

while the air
feels the shivers
of the audacious fatiguing caress

Suddenly in the sky's harem
the black outline
of an enemy trimotor
disturbs provokes
a desire for death revenge
in the excited jealous fighter

Machine-gun belts
d i s c h a r g e
fanning out volleys of lead
to cool the flushed cheeks
of the clouds
that withdraw in fear
to the seats of the sky's
immense stadium
like Vestals with down-turned thumbs[55]

The roar of motors
rebounds around the sky's bowl
like diamond splinters
crushed by gears

The nimble fighter is hit
and gushes petrol

It blanches

With a mighty effort
it soars 100 metres higher
than the enemy trimotor

It hurls itself downward

It s t r i k e s

Violent clash of aluminium
twisted splintered
propellers metal

A giant torch
whistling
s c r e e c h i n g
p l u m m e t i n g
I L L U M I N A T I N G
the evening's hazy warmth
thick with Mediterranean scents

**A THUD**

s s s i l e n c e

Now the grey clouds darken
shedding
loving tears
over the smoking pyre
bathing
the petals of an enamoured rose
that fades
trembling with pleasure

# My dear Brai

I have always seen a secret envy of the dialectical abilities of my beloved Neapolitans sparkling on the tip of your skilfully plied fencer's foil

Now the medical officer Enzo Brai gives voice to the generous heart of a good Roman 'der Cupolone'[56] along the Dalmatian coast

From your medical post admire those sunsets of Pola[57] for me which we once appreciated together (and forget the graceful darting muscles of those magnificent Istrian girls that you wanted to make us believe you had thoroughly enjoyed)

*February 1943*

# To the Sunsets of
# Pola by the Sea

My Futurist heart
wants to blast
into the sunset's corrugated sky
splinters of rubies diamonds
which my youth
embellishes and proffers
with colourful images

Frenzied ambition
to steal
polychrome vibrations
from Pola's sunsets

The motor-boats' propellers
sing a fluid song
steeped in deep blue

Softness of padded forms
that fade in a galaxy
of discoloured pearls
above the languid gulf
violated
by the steel of cruisers

SUNSETS OF POLA
I will exalt you in the poem
burned by my imagination
that savours this moment as
f l e e t i n g
as the transition
between dawn and daybreak

With the lightest of fingers
you transform this mercantile landscape
into a kaleidoscopic perfumed
paradise

Your caresses
tint the windows of houses
as delicately
as the touch of lilac flowers
imparts mist
to the tender face of a child
as velvety as a peach

Bright oranges that
twitch and quiver like
lustfully caressed virgins

Pale pinks

Purples enamelled with silver

One evening
I thirstily drank
a draught of sunlight
which drowned in the sea
its opalescent hues piercing
a rolling panorama softened
by twilight's vapours

The shipyards' chimneys
heedlessly stain
the sky that darkens
with long plumes of smoke

SUNSETS OF POLA
you are like the nostalgia of the soldier
who seems to see again
the longing lips of a beloved woman

This is how I will remember you

And my heart
will burn
the lingering scoria of nostalgia
exalting
the flanks of cruisers
that want to blast
your enchantments
with their 203 guns[58]

A music
of acute angles
and vertical rainbow stripes
announces
the sunset's end

My soul
has split the night
cracking
the dark blue
of the starry sky

# Dear Da Campo

I see you speaking to your soldiers from the S. Marco Battalion with that persuasive voice you used in Florence when we gathered around my bed after the signal for lights-out to speak of the Fatherland of science of women of poetry

A breath of airy Venetian elegance accompanied you wherever you went

You were even refined on that evening of general 'drunkenness' when you stood on your bed and affectionately proclaimed the need to distribute kisses to the lower lateral border of the sternocleidomastoid

Today I send you a kiss seasoned with dust and motors

Pass it on to your little boy who will innocently enjoy the spectacle of gunfire over Naples

*March 1943*

# Tracer Bullets

Dynamic cobweb
against the night's black velvet
catching
tiresome metal flies

Anti-aircraft batteries
launch 100000 tracer bullets
into the sky
crossed strings of an
enticing phosphorescent harp

A snared aircraft's wing
makes them vibrate
composing
a tragic harmony of death

A Futurist child
sweetly claps his little hands
at the firework display's
noisy Catherine-wheel

# My dear Motta

On your face as patient as that of an Indian monk that wants to bewitch the supple elegancies of the Macedonians with large damp mossy eyes I see again the mysterious calm of Brioni[59] which we visited together

Today as Naples stretches out in the sun like a panther with a turbulent heart I point the way towards that island as a path for your casualties of war

*November 1942*

# The Dream Island

Sea of refined oil

Deep blue harmonies
with turquoise veining

My soul
is on the blade of the light hull
that painlessly cuts
the sea's bright silk

Joyful contrast
with the boisterous seaplanes
from Puntisella[60] which arrogantly shatter
the afternoon's peace
wearing huge moustaches of foam

A trimotor approaches

IT LOOMS

**IT ASSAILS US**

with the gusts of its propellers
and greets us
with a youthful throbbing

that makes our light craft
tremble

The sail swells

We moor at a deserted pier
its steps slimy with moss

Infinite peace

B R I O N I

Long bottle-green avenues
trace a straight blue track
on the sky
which begins to be
bathed by the sunset

Arabesques of twilight tones
inspiring sensual dreams

I seem to see
the meadows of Poliziano's *Giostra*[61]
Americanized by golf courses

They say
that on moonlit nights
the forest's virgins
come down to bathe
naked among the rocks
on the backs of spirited horses
while the rhythms
of mournful music float
from the large hotels

Our souls
become crystal cups

misted
by the infinite coloured caresses
of the sunset's soft vapours

We flee
to escape this spell
that wants to make us slumber
e t e r n a l l y

Once more on the tranquil sea
its delicious lunar melancholy
is more enchanting
than the naked sirens of the rocks

I have energized
the sail without wind
and our sleeping hearts
with the internal-combustion engines
of my swift Futurist imagination

# Mother

On an airfield during an hour of peace that anticipates the coming battle I recall those spring afternoons when my infant imagination played beneath your loving eyes on the fresh grass with its clusters of pines

The skinny arms of the fir trees haunted my dreams

Now your heart trembles for our bombarded land and I cradle it in my strong arms to keep it safe

Like every Italian mother your glance contains swathes of shadow that cover me and hold me close yet you bravely let me go knowing that the Great Mother has need of me

Mothers of Italy your sacrifice is greater than that of our lives because it is easier to die than to outlive one's own offspring

*September 1942*

# Waiting on the Field

Siesta of trimotors
digesting
thousands of air miles
bluish storms
the wearisome oscillating caresses
of clouds air pockets

Now they inject
cubic metres of stimulating fuel
impatient
to enjoy
the pangs of speed once more

Intent on swooping down to tickle
the top of that bell-tower
which will writhe about
ding dong dang lang dang
with peals of crystalline laughter

The propellers' breath
plays a green arpeggio
over the meadow's harmony

A splash of sunlight
illuminates
cyclamen notes

# To the Futurist poet Ala[62]

At times life can seem like a rainbow across which one walks passing through grey and coloured bands that the imagination paints with the tones at its disposal

Last year in a grey zone of shared dreams my bloodied heart painted multicoloured streaks with the pastel tones of my beloved Naples so that we might enjoy the many hues of the Venetian lagoon

I no longer dream because my eyes shine like steel in launching their attack on life

But with closed eyes our souls speak in silence caressing flowers

*July 1942*

# Flying over Venice

The lagoon regales us
with a tremulous sunset
of delicate opalescent hues

Mosaic gold
pours from the sun
in a single gush
like a sacred anthem
in this glittering cathedral
bathed in liquid blue

Madonnas' perfumes
and infinite clouds of
tender first communion veils

In the languorous lagoon I sense
your dark eyelashes
kissing your loving
eyes

The caresses of gondolas
full of dreams
twine themselves around your neck
with lunar pendants
and foaming lace

COME

On silver wings
I want to offer you all of Venice
from 3000 metres

A little pearl
with subtle turquoise veining

Now it is a jewel
with a light green filigree
of tiny faceted stones

Place it in your dark hair
kissed by my glance
which the propeller blends
with the sun's vapours

COME

Our paired hearts
have long wings
whose shadows
caress
the shivering water

And with my lips
moist from dreaming of your kisses
I lightly brush your palms
smelling of
stars and lunar forests

# To my dear and glorious Futurist friend Benedetta Marinetti[63]

The bombardments that Naples endures fearless and singing put me in mind of the intense Futurist spirituality of your now celebrated painting *Speed of a Motor-boat* which I admired again recently in Rome's National Gallery of Modern Art

Unlike a traditional artist who would have simply placed a splash of white foam around prow and stern you have immortalized the Gulf as a great aeropainter laying an immense wake of golden lozenges across its cobalt surface to evoke the startling speed of a motor-boat that is already on the horizon and ready to generate new fluid Mediterranean chequerboards of gold and blue

*June 1942*

BENEDETTA
*Speed of a Motor-boat*[64]

# Motor Torpedo-boat

Rumbling of sheet steel
excited by motors

The motor torpedo-boat
slips anchor
with a daring burst of speed

Hurling itself
into the dawn's first mists
that give grey-brown tones
to the salty green sea
wounded by the resonance
of powerful motors

Violently shattering
the bright crystalline slab
which retaliates
spraying splinters
along its hard flanks

The pilot has nailed
his soul to the prow
his nerves to the rudder
his heart to the torpedoes

He has a thirst for glory and vengeance

**ITALY** bellicose music
your motor torpedo-boat of fleshsteel
demands a kiss from you this evening

At anchor
or at the bottom of the sea

# Dear Bandini

Looking through the notes I took in Florence while attending the Medical Officer Training School I come across the following observations

"Bandini is the most respected man in III Company. With his large canvas jacket and high-peaked *bustina*[65] he possesses the characteristic air of an orderly attached to a late 19th-century cavalry officer. He has roguish little moustaches and a charming smile. He is undoubtedly very popular with the women. He pronounces his 'r's in a very soft French manner that reminds me of the trembling of a reed perched on by a love-struck swallow."

I remember your pyjamas as you clambered over the railings to steal a kiss from the mouth of your beautiful naturalized-Florentine Neapolitan lover as the trumpet sounded the signal for lights-out

Now you scrump orange blossoms to perfume your field hospital in the Conca d'Oro[66]

*June 1943*

# Lights-out

Today my soul
sparkles on the Arno

Between the austere arches
of an ancient cloister[67]
a strange melody
takes arcuate form
spiralling in the warm air's
hazy mists
that liquefy
between bridges
resembling beautiful
sleeping women

The melody flares up
bursting from a brass throat
in incandescent blocks
which the evening shatters
p u l v e r i s i n g  i t
in the starry expanse

The Milky Way gleams with it
twinkling like machine-gun fire
raining down
on the serenity of Boboli[68]

A green-brown mystery envelops it
in whispered words of love
the banter of fountains

A heavy velvet cloth
extinguishes little flames
of nostalgia

# Dear Picardi[69]

In the operating theatre a jet of molten gold shaped by your skilful hands seems to pour down from the large lamp onto the faces of the wounded

Your soulful fingers patiently work on war-torn flesh and monsters of deformed skin and bone are once more transformed into human beings

And my heart which throbs close by as I pass your surgical instruments to you amidst the blood and the stench of medicine feels as pure and as light as if it were floating freely on a parachute in the morning air that scents the Neapolitan landscape

*June 1943*

# Parachutist

My grey-green uniform[70]
turns blue as I plummet
acrobatically
with joy as boundless
as the cerulean void
that surrounds me

Anticipation of the leap

The trimotor sings
muffled echoes of melodies
and rains white rose petals
which adorn the sky

Finally my ambitious nerves
dominate space

Furtively stealing
a sunbeam
to prick
the low clouds
that scatter

The millennial pride
of atmospheric atoms
batters the heavy silk

of my parachute
condensing again and again

The enemy would like to nail me
to a star
with exploding words in freedom
redolent of
lead and cypress trees

And I a celestial rose
beflower a green meadow
outstretched arms
Sunday excursions

New mechanized poetry

The turbulent blood
of a Futurist aeropoet
inflames for you
with the endlessly echoing
howling joy
of **REBIRTH**

# Dear Buccafusca[71]

You too are a surgeon and a Futurist poet as well as a mountaineer an aeropainter and above all a Neapolitan

From a torpedo-boat on which I am serving as a war correspondent with our friend Scrivo and his 'Ala' Agency[72] I am enjoying a nocturnal Neapolitan moment which I am sending to you on the radio waves of my poetry

Store it at 40° below zero or hurl it into the Don

It will arrive it has already reached[73] your Angelina with all the colours of the sunset

*April 1942*

# Night Space

NIGHT SPACE
plush sea of black velvet
its sands shrill
with silver fanfares

YOUR LOVE
a throbbing of weightless atoms
on your violet eyelashes

MY LOVE
colours life
with the rosy hues of your skin

YOUR LIPS
two pieces of coral in a drop of light

MY DREAMS
incandescent wings hooked to the stars

MY DESIRE
to become a musical note

# My dear Nuti

My spirit was put to the test by our hurried ascent of Costa S. Giorgio in Florence[74] after a six-hour march although I tried to refresh myself by gazing into your eyes as green as Capri's grotto[75]

You wanted to soften the clamorous military atmosphere with your aspirate Sienese 'H' as deep as the breath of the sea on moonlit nights

Yet it was beautiful to fortify one's muscles and one's heart by thirstily imbibing the Florentine dawn

*January 1943*

# Marching at Dawn

Powerful October sky
polished by the moon
vying with the stars'
sparkling geometry

The Arno is a mirror
misted by the night's breath

THE BATTALION MARCHES

Daybreak's freshness
starts to fade
the silent shadows
outlined by the moon

On the sky's heavy
dark blue ice
dawn – divine skater –
rises on butterfly wings
enveloped in a grey-pink haze

Kissing her bare shoulders
leaves a salty taste

Mellow waves of pale violet
with the softness of adolescent lips

A red circle with swelling rings
embraces clasps the earth
which smells
of moss of grass of dew

Weakened by the grip
it blanches
and fades to fresh light greens
that slowly drown
in blue depths

THE BATTALION MARCHES

I want to quench my soul's thirst
at this dawn as sharp
as our bayonets

Shivering air
and the brutal silhouettes
of steeples towers cypresses

Florence is a grey curl
in the dark green hair
that flows down the mountains of the Casentino[76]

Two small clouds
bow in prayer
before the dazzling sun
admiring itself now
in the brown steel
of our rifles

# Dear Busnardo

The memory of your pure soul spiralling upwards on crystal steps helps me to find strength in my pain

To escape the terrible devastation of our adored Italy through Art and through Love so as to be reborn purified

I can see you with your scalpel skilfully engraving the carnal blueness of the sky with white notes that rain from the moon in a musical cascade of stars

In them I hear the echo of a Naples of days gone by which must re-emerge strengthened by powerful electric dreams to become the Mediterranean beacon of a renewed Italy

*August 1943*

# Optimism

The bitter mouth
savours lacerating joys
that give pain

Madness of cosmic speeds

Listen to the stars

Harmony of spheres

The heart is on the rocks of INFINITY

Shadows tremble
tonight on the Arno
pained by tears of light

# Dear Signora Hilde

Your eyes fixed on the blue sash of my Medical Officer of the Watch uniform sparkling like a dawn of golden shooting stars above the Gulf of Naples

You made me savour the profile of the weary mountains dozing at sunset

To scale them and reach summits of joy in the fresh morning air

This evening your mountains' fir trees kiss the stars

*April 1943*

# Morning

The mountains of Trentino
chilled by the night
wrap themselves in the lake's veil
while the sun
ignites their peaks
like immense beacons
to illuminate the day

Power of rock
sculpted by time

The hedgerows wear ermine cloaks

The morning light
burns in your hair

# Salvatore Gulisano
# Tank officer
## Killed in action at El Alamein[77]

Loving Italy war your woman like torrents of Vesuvian lava

On the turret of your tank you offered up all of your dreams so that your already intoxicated scorched blood might imbibe a green Mediterranean breath

The oceanic chorus of the Egyptian sands raises a pyramid to the glory of your twenty years in fluttering colours of heroism

Your beautiful death is an eternal youth

**Salvatore Gulisano**

*July 1943*

# Joy

The universe
is a flux
of atoms in love

A rosebud
explodes with colourful splinters
and the most delicate perfumes

Motors howl
in their desire
to bite the stars

Triangular souls
are projected into the blue
creating
noisy spaces
and musical architectures

I want to cry **ITALY**
with my chest torn open by a bomb
then dance crazily
on the sun's spokes
to m e r g e  m y s e l f
with I N F I N I T Y

# Endnotes

1   An honorific denoting the Futurist leader's status as an *Accademico d'Italia* (member of the Italian Royal Academy, a body to which he was appointed in 1929).

2   After 1938, Marinetti preferred the more technical sounding term *collaudo* to that of 'introduction' or 'preface'. See Glauco Viazzi, 'F. T. Marinetti collaudatore', in F. T. Marinetti, *Collaudi futuristi*, ed. by Glauco Viazzi (Naples: Guida, 1977), pp. 5-16 (p. 7).

3   Emilio Buccafusca (1913-1990) was a poet and painter who first encountered Marinetti in 1931; he went on to become a key figure in Neapolitan Futurist circles. Having studied medicine, he served for a time at the Italian military hospital in Voroshilovgrad (modern-day Luhansk in eastern Ukraine) during World War Two, in addition to various other locations in the region. See also below, p. 87.

4   Gomel is a city in the south-east of modern-day Belarus. Buccafusca's characterization of Kolomea (modern-day Kolomyia in the Ukraine) is both poignant and chilling, given that by late 1942 the occupying Nazi forces had largely completed their grim task of exterminating the local Jewish population by means of deportations to death camps and summary executions *in situ*.

5   My italics. An untranslatable expression, conveying Buccafusca's profound admiration for the Futurist leader.

6   Giuseppe Casciaro (1863-1941) was a painter and pastellist whose works often depicted Neapolitan landscapes.

7   An asterism in the northern celestial hemisphere.

8   A strong, cool, north-easterly wind that blows through the Mediterranean.

9   My italics. Marinetti's use of this spelling, instead of the more conventional *lacrime*, may indicate a punning reference to *Lágrima* (*Teardrop*), a famous composition by the Spanish guitarist Francisco Tárrega (1852-1909).

10  My italics. A *scugnizzo* is a Neapolitan street urchin.

11  Presumably a reference to characters from Torquato Tasso's epic poem *Jerusalem Delivered* (1581), and the Ottoman Suleiman the Magnificent.

12  My italics. Three instruments used in popular Neapolitan music, being particularly

associated with the city's 'Piedigrotta' festival. Marinetti described their characteristics in his manifesto 'Dynamic and Synoptic Declamation' (1916), in Lawrence Rainey, Christine Poggi and Laura Wittman, eds, *Futurism: An Anthology* (New Haven and London: Yale University Press, 2009), pp. 219-24 (pp. 222-23).

13   The Italian *fianchi* is used to denote both flanks (of a hill or mountain) and hips – a double meaning that Marinetti exploits here.

14   My italics. Typically associated with the Carnival of Venice, the *bautta* is a half-mask worn with a short black cape and tricorn hat.

15   See below, p. 78.

16   Enrico Prampolini (see above, p. 3) was a frequent visitor to Capri following his first trip in 1922, when he painted a famous image of the island's Blue Grotto. The *bagnante caprese* mentioned by Marinetti here may be a reference to Prampolini's portrait of Adriana Capocci di Belmonte (*Solar Spatiality*; or, *Adriana in Capri*) of 1941-42.

17   A smokeless propellant made from nitrocellulose and nitroglycerine.

18   My italics.

19   The festival of St Lucy (from the Latin *lux*, meaning 'light') takes place between 12 and 13 December each year.

20   S. Lucia a Mare was completely destroyed by an Allied air raid on 4 August 1943. It is unclear if Marinetti's *collaudo* was written before or after this event; as the date of Bellanova's 'letter' to Busnardo indicates (see below, p. 92) work on *Bombarded Naples Sings* was still underway in the immediate lead up to its publication in August 1943.

21   St Januarius is the patron saint of Naples. One of the city's most precious religious relics is a phial supposedly containing his dried blood, which 'miraculously' liquefies three times each year.

22   My italics. Italian character or sentiment.

23   Codified by Marinetti in 1921, 'Tactilism' was a form of artistic expression that relied entirely on touch for its effects, eschewing any visual or verbal dimensions. See F. T. Marinetti, 'Tactilism', in Rainey, Poggi and Wittman, *Futurism: An Anthology*, cit., pp. 264-69.

24   A key figure in the cultural life of Naples, Gaspare Casella (1882-1962) followed his father into the book business, and was a keen admirer of Futurism. Marinetti's comparison of him to Molo Beverello reflects not only the proximity of the Libreria Casella to that busy port, but also neatly conveys the image of a bustling and continuous exchange of literary goods and ideas. In 1943 Casella's bookshop in Piazza Municipio was destroyed by aerial bombardment. Marinetti intended to republish the present *collaudo* under the title *L'editore Casella sotto le bombe* (*Casella the Publisher Beneath the Bombs*), but due to the war the volume never entered production. On Casella see Matteo D'Ambrosio, *Futurismo a Napoli. Indagini e documenti* (Naples, Liguori, 1995).

25   A poet, journalist and satirical novelist, Anatole France (1844-1924) was awarded the Nobel Prize for Literature in 1921. Like Casella, he was the son of a bookseller.

26 "This word [...] embraces a huge variety of nuts and edible seeds of all kinds, many of them strange in appearance [...]. Nothing of this collection of edible trifles [...] can be said to have much taste, but chewing them promotes reflection." Norman Lewis, *Naples '44: An Intelligence Officer in the Italian Labyrinth* (London: Eland, 2002), p. 86.

27 D'Ambrosio has noted how here and elsewhere "the names of those who frequented [Casella's shop] appear: Futurists, politicians, journalists, intellectuals" (*Futurismo a Napoli*, cit., p. 246). In this particular passage, these would appear to be: Giovanni Treccani degli Alfieri (1877-1961) an industrialist, publisher and developer of the renowned, eponymous, encyclopaedia; Cornelio Di Marzio (1896-1944) a Fascist politician, intellectual and President of the Confederation of Professionals and Artists; Alberto Pariani (1876-1955) a military general and bibliophile; Giuseppe Bastianini (1899-1961) a Fascist politician and diplomat.

28 Texts by various authors and poets associated with Futurism: Edwin Cerio (1875-1960) *Aria di Capri. Vol. I – Il libro degli uomini* (1935); Benedetta (1897-1977) *Astra e il sottomarino. Vita trasognata* (1935); Francesco Cangiullo (1884-1977) *Piedigrotta. Parolinlibertà* (1916), *Caffèconcerto. Alfabeto a sorpresa* [1919], *Poesia Pentagrammata* (1923), *Le Serate Futuriste* [1930]; Giovanni Acquaviva (1900-1971) *L'essenza del futurismo suo poetico dinamismo italiano fra le filosofie* (1941); Gaetano Pattarozzi (1914-1959) *Aeropoema futurista della Sardegna* [1939]; Bruno Giordano Sanzin (1906-1994) *Ottimismo ad ogni costo* (1938); Castrense Civello (1909-1982) *Aria Madre. Glorificazione dell'aviazione italiana in versi liberi e parole in libertà* (1941); Giacomo Giardina (1903-1994) *Quand'ero pecoraio. Liriche* (1931); Ignazio Scurto (1912-1954) *L'Aeroporto* (1939); Geppo Tedeschi (1907-1993) *Corti circuiti* (1938); Bruno Corra (1892-1976) *Il Toro. Romanzo d'avventure e d'amore del tempo dei Borgia* [1922]; Pino Masnata (1901-1968) *Poesia dei ferri chirurgici* [1940]. Cangiullo was an exponent of Futurist 'synthetic theatre', writing brief vignettes for the stage, and was also the co-author (with Marinetti) of the manifesto 'The Theatre of Surprise' (1921). However, Cammarota lists no volume by Cangiullo titled *Teatro sintetico* in his 2006 bibliography of Futurist writers; neither is there an entry for Libero Russo. As D'Ambrosio has noted, Marinetti's reference to the latter's 'French Poems' presumably relates to an anthology of verse written by a Neapolitan poet associated with Futurism named Luigi Libero Russo (dates unknown) titled *La cité des colombes* (1938). See his entry on this figure in Ezio Godoli, ed., *Il dizionario del futurismo*, 2 vols (Florence: Vallecchi; Rovereto: MART, 2001).

29 On *Nose-diving into Love*, see above, pp. 7-8. Marinetti's identification of a sense of continuity between that text and *Bombarded Naples Sings* is somewhat perplexing, as the two books are very different in tone and form.

30 See above, pp. 7-8.

31 See below, p. 46.

32 Marinetti erroneously refers to one of Boccioni's lost plaster sculptures here; in fact it was the iconic *Unique Forms of Continuity in Space* (1913) that was cast in bronze by the Fonderia Chiurazzi of Naples. See Luigi Sansone, 'Le sculture in gesso di Umberto

Boccioni: storie e documenti inediti', in Volker W. Feierabend, ed., *Umberto Boccioni. La rivoluzione della scultura / Die Revolution der Skulptur* (Milan: Silvana; Frankfurt: VAF Fondazione, 2006), pp. 24-63 (pp. 40-50).

33 Aside from the erstwhile Futurist writer Aldo Palazzeschi (1885-1974), I have been unable to discover – with any certainty – information regarding the other figures referred to in this section. 'Comisso' was presumably the writer Giovanni Comisso (1895-1969) and 'Giusso' was probably the critic Lorenzo Giusso, while 'Chuzeville' may have been the writer and translator Jean Chuzeville (1886-1962).

34 Other minor political and cultural figures of the day.

35 The idea for a 'National Gallery of Futurist Art' would appear to date back to the autumn of 1941. On 12 October, Luigi Scrivo's ALA press agency (see above, p. 23, n. 43) issued a statement announcing the establishment of a private gallery dedicated to the movement (the word 'museum' was studiously avoided, for obvious reasons) in Marinetti's home at Piazza Adriana 11, Rome. Its collection consisted predominantly of recent works, although it was noted that "a room has been reserved for works by the masters of pictorial Futurism: Boccioni, Sant'Elia, Balla, Russolo, Severini, Carrà, Soffici, Funi, Sironi". 'F. T. Marinetti fonda in Roma la prima galleria d'aeropittura' (Cra.2.210). In a letter of 23 June 1943, the Futurist leader claimed that the plan to make this private gallery the basis for a national public collection was subsequently "willed and authorized by the Duce while I was fighting as a volunteer in Russia" – that is, at some point between July and November 1942 (GRI 850702 / S. III, B. 8, F. 10, p. 5). And indeed, the project appears to have been officially announced by the regime through its own favoured public relations agency, the Agenzia Stefani, in early 1943; see Mino Somenzi, 'La galleria nazionale d'arte futurista e aeropittura di guerra approvata dal Duce, sintetizzerà la poesia e tutte le arti italiane novatrici', in *Autori e Scrittori*, February 1943, pp. 1-2 (Cra.3.17). Ultimately, this project never materialized since "after World War II the new Republican State declared Mussolini's commitments null and void" (Giovanni Lista, *Futurism* (Paris: Terrail, 2001), p. 200).

36 A nickname by which Emilio Buccafusca was known.

37 One of the most famous hotels on the city's Left Bank, frequented by artists and writers. One such guest was James Joyce, who write part of *Ulysses* there. According to D'Ambrosio, the Parisian sojourn mentioned here took place in 1938, on which occasion Casella, Marinetti and Buccafusca visited the painter Wassily Kandinsky in his studio (*Futurismo a Napoli*, cit., p. 246).

38 My italics. The opening lines of *Tarantellucia*, a popular Neapolitan song written in local dialect by Ernesto Murolo (1876-1939).

39 Stéphane Mallarmé (1842-1898) was a French Symbolist poet; the striking typographical arrangements of his famous text *Un Coup de dés* (1897) anticipated many of the formal innovations made by the twentieth-century literary avant gardes. Louis Aragon (1897-1982) and André Breton (1896-1966) were both leading figures of the Surrealist

movement.

40 François Rabelais (c.1483/94-1553) was a French writer renowned for his robust – and frequently bawdy – writings.

41 My italics; my use of French. At the Battle of Waterloo, General Pierre Cambronne (1770-1842) is supposed disdainfully to have replied "Shit!" to the call for his surrender. The phrase *le mot de Cambronne* subsequently came to be used as a polite euphemism.

42 Mandin (1872-1943) was murdered at the hands of Nazi forces in Sonnenburg concentration camp around two months before the present text was published. It is unclear if Marinetti knew of his fate at the time of writing.

43 The oldest extant fortification in Naples, the Castel dell'Ovo takes its name from a legend that the Roman poet Virgil had placed a magic egg in the structure's foundations (or had hidden it somewhere within the building, according to different versions of the story), prophesying that disaster would befall the city should the egg ever break.

44 Presumably a reference to the use of Verona green by early Renaissance artists to underpaint flesh tones.

45 See above, p. 10.

46 During the Second World War, Marinetti sent postcards bearing the slogan *Adorare l'Italia* to members of his movement *en masse*. See Tullio Crali, 'Una vita per il Futurismo. Tra scossoni e vuoti d'aria alla ricerca di quota', in Claudio Rebeschini, ed., *Crali aeropittore futurista*, exh. cat. (Milan: Electa, 1994), pp. 143-267 (pp. 171-72). On Marinetti's wartime exploits in the Soviet Union, see below, n. 52.

47 Gerardo Dottori (1884-1977), *Aerial Battle above the Gulf of Naples; or, Inferno of Aerial Battle above the Paradise of the Gulf*, 1942, oil on board, 200 x 150 cm, Milan: private collection (courtesy of the Archivio Gerardo Dottori Associazione Culturale). A pioneer of both aeropainting and Futurist sacred art, Dottori aligned himself with Marinetti's movement around 1912 and went on to become the most significant representative of Futurism in Umbria.

48 Given that Vesuvius was to erupt in March 1944, seriously damaging around 80 aircraft of the USAAF's 340th Bombardment Group based at Pompeii Airfield, Bellanova's poem seems remarkably prescient.

49 Augusto Mario Platone (1912-1941) became involved with Turin's Futurist group in 1931, and served as editor of the journal *Stile Futurista* between 1934 and 1935. He participated in Italy's disastrous invasion of Greece (October 1940), falling in battle on the slopes of Mount Golico in Albania on 7 March 1941. Subsequently, he became something of a Futurist icon – as witnessed by the hagiographic tone of Bellanova's prose – and two Futurist groups were named in his honour. The gold medal mentioned in the title of this 'letter' seems to refer to the *Medaglia d'Oro al Valor Militare*, awarded to soldiers for outstanding acts of bravery and courage. However, it would appear that this was never conferred on Platone (see http://www.quirinale.it/elementi/onorificenze.aspx for a full list of recipients [accessed 25 November 2016]) which may explain why Bellanova awards

him another, on behalf of the Futurist movement, at the end of this piece. An eye-witness account of Platone's death can be found in Antonio Ferrante di Ruffano, *Never Retreat: The Memoirs of an Uncompromising Alpine Soldier*, 2nd edn (London: The Private Library, 2011), pp. 63-64.

50    Antonio Sant'Elia (1888-1916) was the most significant Futurist architect during the 'heroic' years of the movement, prior to World War One.

51    To commemorate Platone's death, Marinetti issued a volume of his writings in 1941 titled *Man and the Machine* (*L'uomo e la macchina*).

52    Marinetti volunteered for military service in the Soviet Union during the Second World War, departing for the front (at the age of sixty-five, and in poor health) from Verona's Porta Nuova railway station on 27 July 1942. He finally arrived at his destination – Kantemirovka, near the River Don – on 16 August. There, he served with the rank of *Primo Seniore* (equivalent to Lieutenant Colonel) in the '23 Marzo' unit of the Militia. On 12 September he participated in a successful military operation to recapture the village of Sviniuka from Soviet troops. However, the increasingly cold weather compelled the frail Futurist leader to return to Italy on 5 November. Marinetti recounted his experiences in a poetic work titled *Originalità russa di masse distanze radiocuori* (Rome: Voland, 1996) and in the final lecture he would deliver at the Italian Royal Academy, on 11 January 1943. See Gino Agnese, *Marinetti. Una vita esplosiva* (Milan: Camunia, 1990), pp. 284-96, and Matteo D'Ambrosio, 'Marinetti al fronte russo', in Matteo D'Ambrosio, *Futurismo e altre avanguardie* (Naples: Liguori, 1999), pp. 39-69. World War Two was indeed the fifth conflict in which Marinetti had participated, having served as war correspondent for a Parisian newspaper during Italy's Libyan campaign of 1911, and witnessing the Siege of Adrianople the following year during the First Balkan War; he subsequently saw active service in World War One and the Italian invasion of Ethiopia (1935-36).

53    *Marinetti at the Front*, c. 1942, tempera on board, 33 x 41 cm, private collection (reproduced by kind permission of the artist's heirs).

54    *Motor, Seducer of Clouds*, 1939, oil on board, 142 x 120 cm, private collection (reproduced by kind permission of the artist's heirs).

55    Bellanova uses the term *pollice verso* – a gesture used by Roman spectators at gladiatorial contests.

56    A dialectal reference to the large cupola of St Peter's Basilica.

57    Pula in modern-day Croatia, at the southern tip of the Istrian peninsula.

58    The 203mm/53 Ansaldo was the main battery gun of Italy's most advanced heavy cruisers during World War Two.

59    Brijuni in modern-day Croatia, off the southern tip of the Istrian peninsula. Famed for their scenic beauty, its islands are now a national park.

60    Puntižela in modern-day Croatia.

61    My italics. Poliziano was the *nom de plume* of Angelo Ambrogini (1454-1494), a poet of the Italian Renaissance. His most famous work, *Stanze per la giostra*, recounts the Florentine

tournament of 1475 and the exploits of its victor, Giuliano de' Medici.

62    Little is known of Alaide Numerico, a poet associated with Rome's Futurist circles. In January 1941 she and Bellanova recited their poems at an event held at the city's Hostaria dell'Orso (see above, p. 9, Fig. 2).

63    A poet and painter, Benedetta Cappa (1897-1977) met Marinetti in the studio of Giacomo Balla in 1918; she and the Futurist leader married in 1923.

64    Benedetta, *Speed of a Motor-boat*, 1923-24, oil on canvas, 70 x 110 cm, Rome: Galleria d'Arte Moderna di Roma Capitale (© Roma Capitale; reproduced with permission).

65    My italics. A type of military beret or cap.

66    A plain in the north-western region of Sicily surrounding Palermo.

67    The Scuola di Applicazione di Sanità Militare had barracks in two former convents on Florence's steep Costa San Giorgio in the city's Oltrarno district, near the Ponte Vecchio and Forte di Belvedere.

68    A reference to the famous sixteenth-century gardens at Palazzo Pitti in Florence.

69    Prof. Giovanni Picardi (1906-1975) was an eminent Italian surgeon. An overview of his career can be found in Nicola Picardi, *Ricordo della vita di Giovanni Picardi 1906-1975* (Villanova di Castenaso: Leonelli Printing, 2006).

70    *Grigioverde* was the name given to Italian military uniforms.

71    See above, n. 3.

72    See above, p. 23, n. 43.

73    In accordance with Futurist theory, Bellanova here juxtaposes different verb tenses to convey the immediacy of radio communication.

74    See above, n. 67.

75    A reference to the Grotta Verde on the south of the island.

76    A densely-forested valley in Tuscany.

77    Second Lieutenant Salvatore Gulisano was killed on 31 October 1942 while serving in the 133rd Armoured Division ('Littorio'). An account of his death can be found in Dino Campini, *El Alamein. I carri della Littorio* (n. p.: Italia Storica E-book, 2015), n. p. (section 17).

# Selected Bibliography

## Archival Sources and Abbreviations

**Cra.**
Denotes sources from the Fondo Tullio Crali, stored at the Archivio del'900, Museo di Arte Moderna e Contemporanea di Trento e Rovereto (MART), Rovereto. The prefix is followed by two figures: the first identifies the volume in which the item is located; the second identifies the number of the item itself.

**GRI**
Denotes sources from the Getty Research Institute, Los Angeles. The prefix is followed by the number of the archive; three additional figures identify the S.[eries], B.[ox] and F.[older] in which the item is located.

## Books and Exhibition Catalogues

**Bellanova**, Piero, *Bombardata Napoli canta* (Rome: Edizioni Futuriste di 'Poesia', 1943)
— *Picchiata nell'amore* (Rome: Unione Editoriale d'Italia, 1940)
**Berghaus**, Günter, *Italian Futurist Theatre 1909-1944* (Oxford: Clarendon Press, 1998)
— *Futurism and Politics: Between Anarchist Rebellion and Fascist Reaction, 1909-1944* (Providence and Oxford: Berghahn, 1996)
**Bohn**, Willard, ed., *Italian Futurist Poetry* (Toronto, Buffalo and New York: University of Toronto Press, 2005)
**Cammarota**, Domenico, *Futurismo. Bibliografia di 500 scrittori italiani* (Milan: Skira; Rovereto: MART, 2006)

**Cappelli**, Vittorio, ed., *Futurismo calabrese. Poesie, tavole parolibere, sintesi teatrali* (Soveria Mannelli: Rubbettino, 1997)

**Cappelli**, Vittorio, and Luciano Caruso, eds, *Calabria futurista. Documenti, immagini, opere*, exh. cat. (Soveria Mannelli: Rubbettino, 1997)

**D'Ambrosio**, Matteo, *Futurismo a Napoli. Indagini e documenti* (Naples: Liguori, 1995)

**Duci**, Mirella, ed., *Fondo Tullio Crali. Inventario* (Rovereto: Nicolodi; MART, 2008)

**Giuliani**, Gianna, *Le strisce interiori. Cinema italiano e psicoanalisi* (Rome: Bulzoni, 1980)

**Godoli**, Ezio, ed., *Il dizionario del futurismo*, 2 vols (Florence: Vallecchi; Rovereto: MART, 2001)

**Marinetti**, F. T., *Collaudi futuristi*, ed. by Glauco Viazzi (Naples: Guida, 1977)

**Marinetti**, F. T., and others, eds, *Canzoniere futurista amoroso guerriero* (Savona: Istituto Grafico Brizio, 1943)

**Salaris**, Claudia, *Storia del futurismo. Libri giornali manifesti*, 2nd rev. edn (Rome: Riuniti, 1992)

**Tarsitano**, Umberto, *Linee del Romanzo futurista sintetico nel percorso letterario di Piero Bellanova* (n. p.: n. pub.[ e-book], 2000)

## Essays and Manifestos

**Marinetti**, F. T., 'Tumultuosa serata al Teatro Argentina di Roma in difesa del primato teatrale italiano', in F. T. Marinetti, *Il teatro futurista* (Naples: CLET, 1941), pp. 3-4

**Marinetti**, F. T., Luigi Scrivo and Piero Bellanova, 'L'arte tipografica di guerra e dopoguerra. Manifesto futurista' (1942); repr. in Luciano Caruso, ed., *Manifesti, proclami, interventi e documenti teorici del futurismo 1909-1944*, 4 vols (Florence: SPES-Salimbeni, 1980), vol. III, no. 298

— 'Il romanzo sintetico. Manifesto futurista', in *Il Giornale d'Italia*, 24 December 1939; repr. in Caruso, *Manifesti*, cit., vol. III, no. 297.

**Verdone**, Mario, 'Memoria su Piero Bellanova e "La piccola città" di Thornton Wilder', in Mario Verdone, *Drammaturgia e arte totale. L'avanguardia internazionale – Autori, teorie, opere*, ed. by Rocco Mario Morano (Soveria Mannelli: Rubbettino, 2005), pp. 71-78

Lightning Source UK Ltd.
Milton Keynes UK
UKIC03n2049190818
327440UK00005B/74